Playing with Gender

Playing *with* Gender

A Renaissance Pursuit

EDITED BY

*Jean R. Brink, Maryanne C. Horowitz,
and Allison P. Coudert*

UNIVERSITY OF ILLINOIS PRESS
Urbana and Chicago

This book is printed on acid-free paper.

Library of Congress Cataloging-in-Publication Data

Playing with gender : A Renaissance pursuit / edited by Jean R. Brink,
   Maryanne C. Horowitz, and Allison P. Coudert.
        p.   cm.
   Includes bibliographical references and index.
   ISBN 0-252-01764-1
   1. European literature—Renaissance, 1450–1600—History and
criticism.   2. Sex roles in literature.   3. Amazons in literature.
4. Hermaphroditism in literature.   5. Metamorphosis in literature.
I. Brink, J. R. II. Horowitz, Maryanne Cline, 1945–   .
III. Coudert, Allison, 1941–   .
PN721.P55 1991
809'.933538'09031—dc20   90-41889
                                                               CIP

Contents

Acknowledgments

We would like to express our gratitude to Arizona State University for supporting the annual meetings of the Renaissance Society of America (1987) and the Sixteenth Century Studies Conference (1987). These essays are revised versions of papers presented at those conferences.

Playing with Gender: A Renaissance Pursuit was brought to fruition because of the remarkable talent and industry of Walter von Reinhart, the program coordinator at the Arizona Center for Medieval and Renaissance Studies. Mr. von Reinhart contributed substantially to and supervised every aspect of the publication process, working closely with the contributors and editors. He has been ably assisted by Ms. Whitney A. Peterson, who served as a patient proofreader and who helped prepare the index for this volume. Dr. Daniel T. Brink graciously lent his computer expertise to this project. Our appreciation extends to the conscientious and cordial staff of the University of Illinois Press.

Introduction:
Playing with Gender

MARYANNE CLINE HOROWITZ

This book is a collection of original essays invited to elucidate a major *topos* of Renaissance culture—playing with gender. The volume as a whole provides literary and artistic evidence that the much-acclaimed Renaissance self-fashioning goes hand in hand with playful and creative experimentation with gender distinctions.[1] Our essayists analyze the fashioning of the gendered self in Renaissance imaginary literature and drama, in woodcuts and portraits, and in individual self-imaging.

A specific goal of this three-part, innovative volume is to expand scholarly awareness of three personae that inhabit the Renaissance imagination—the "other,"[2] the Amazon,[3] and the hermaphrodite.[4] First, the seven case studies of texts and images collectively suggest that a crucial aspect of Renaissance fashioning of self is the refashioning of others. Second, in the Renaissance cross-cultural questioning of gender categories, authors and artists enjoy playing with Amazons and other ancient figures who transcend accepted gender stereotypes. An apparently amusing "male" game, presented for the enjoyment of conventional men and women (as in Shakespeare's *Taming of the Shrew*), is refashioning autonomous female figures along traditional gender lines, that is, appropriating them to conserve the status quo. Third, envisioning the hermaphrodite (a being both male and female) becomes a serious spiritual quest for ultimate unity as well as an amusing transvestite game.

Displaying an interest in the social and ideational construction of gender identity and an awareness of the subtle ways in which the writing and reading of literature transform perceptions of gender difference, the authors use "gender" as a category of literary, artistic, and historical analysis.[5] Certain studies focus as much on males adopting conventionally "feminine" roles as on females exhibiting conventionally masculine behavior: for example, Nancy Gutierrez discloses the witchlike behavior of Shakespeare's Iago, Susanne Woods suggests Spenser's self-identification with the Amazon Radigund, and Margaret Sullivan analyzes Sidney's problems in completing the narrative wherein Pyrocles is disguised as an Amazon. Both the idea of the Amazon and the idea of the hermaphrodite derive from male-authored ancient texts, although Renaissance men sometimes think they "see" Amazons in Indians from the Americas and in educated or ruling women in European courts. Because the Renaissance texts and images discussed in this volume are male-authored (although not without female influence and female audience), this collection primarily elucidates male ideals, fantasies, and fears about sexuality and gender.

Indeed, this volume demonstrates that literary analysis of Renaissance men's representations of and fantasies about persons conventionally and unconventionally gendered can contribute fresh insights to the growing interdisciplinary fields of Renaissance studies, women's studies, men's studies, and gender studies. Literary critics have proven to be particularly adept at analyzing the surprising and often subtle ways in which Renaissance texts highlight the nuances of human gendered behavior. The three sections of this volume—"Fashioning the Self and the Other," "Refashioning Gender: Appropriating the Amazon," and "Envisioning the Hermaphrodite"—focus on Renaissance attempts to explore the problematical "in-between" in the social constructs of "masculinity" and "femininity" and in the differentiation of the sexes. The Amazon and the hermaphrodite raise these two distinct issues: the Amazon, as a female who is socialized by an all-female society to adopt some stereotypically "masculine" traits, raises issues of gender construction; the hermaphrodite, a being both male and female, raises issues of sex differentiation as well as of gender construction.

The Renaissance fascination with portrayals of Amazons, including domestication of Amazons and the disguise of men as Amazons, reflects awareness of and curiosity about willful gender transformation. Although self-mutilation of one breast is the extent to which ancient Amazons are "desexed," the image does arouse fear that gender transformation is desexing; after all, Amazons traditionally limit their sexual encounters to procreation. However, Renaissance literary texts that fantasize pursuit of an Amazon for marriage assure those frightened by female independence that even an Amazon can become a conventional woman.

To some extent, the Amazon's combination of autonomous, courageous masculinity with sexually alluring femininity provides a model for androgyny, one that might inspire identification in men or women so inclined; nevertheless, the more complete Renaissance representation of androgyny is the hermaphrodite. Although a sexual aberration, this merger of masculine and feminine traits is so extraordinary that it can be a model for royalty, combining as it does those "paternal" and "maternal" qualities desirable in a just, yet merciful, ruler.

To Renaissance thinkers, the hermaphrodite raises fundamental issues in natural philosophy on the embryonic origins of sex differentiation and the possibilities of sex transformation. The ancient myth of Hermaphroditus tells how the son of Hermes and Aphrodite is joined to the nymph Salmacis in one simultaneously male and female body. In Renaissance medical literature, the hermaphrodite is a human being who develops both male and female genitalia. He/she appears in popular pamphlets of prodigies, in medical textbooks, and in legal documents. He/she is required to become eventually either "he" or "she" before the law. Hermaphrodites challenge not only gender construction but also the classification by sex fundamental to the patriarchal functioning of the Renaissance family, church, and state. They appear to corroborate the accidental nature of sex designation asserted in Aristotelian and Galenic biological theories, which view female and male as polar opposites on a continuum from weakness to strength and which accept that monstrosities occur in nature.

The interest in hermaphrodites displayed in Renaissance discourse suggests that Renaissance individuals link androgyny with the possibility of sex doubling and sex transformation and face a deep ambiguity in confronting the social construction of gender. Playwrights writing for theatrical performances in which men play all the roles epitomize the Renaissance fascination with gendering character and behavior. In fact, the growing opposition to theater in seventeenth-century England may reflect a fear that men effeminizing themselves on stage will infect the audience with similar transformations. The protests are symptomatic of popular, as well as learned, fears of becoming transformed demonically or magically into werewolf, witch, or, alas, woman. Yet as we recall Bottom metamorphosed into an ass in *A Midsummer Night's Dream,* we need no reminder that the fear of metamorphosis is also a subject for mockery and good humor. Indeed, Reginald Scott and Michel de Montaigne in the 1580s apply their wit to undermining the dubious evidence of transformations of humans into witches or werewolves.[6]

The three personae of "other," Amazon, and hermaphrodite illustrate the complexity, paradoxical ambiguity, and ambivalence of "playing." The diversity of our seven authors' theoretical perspectives encourages readers to judge for themselves to what extent the Renaissance flair for playing with gender is a serious intellectual query, good civilized fun, a libidinal release, a nasty game in the perennial war of the sexes, a sign of gender categories in transformation, or an aspect of humanist wit.

J. Huizinga's classic work, *Homo Ludens: A Study of the Play-Element in Culture,* reminds us that studying human history as a record of "players" helps in understanding "how far culture itself bears the character of play."[7] Natalie Z. Davis's historical-anthropological studies of topsy-turvy play, women on top, carnival, masks, and misrule have brought new interdisciplinary skills to the examination of the ritual occasions when the conventional rules of sixteenth-century society were reversed or transformed. Going beyond Huizinga's examples of play and recognizing the ritual in the repetitive scripts of literature, we draw attention to the Renaissance reenactment of stories about Amazon queens or about the son of the goddess of love who became a son-daughter, that is, Hermaphroditus. Artists and authors toy with these figures in what is clearly a titillating pastime—a form, in fact, of erotic pursuit!

Indeed, as this volume establishes, it would not be unusual for an individual living in Europe in the fourteenth, fifteenth, or sixteenth centuries to attend theater that likens the world to a stage, to entice and caress a beloved in a myriad of circuitous acts of courtship, and to appear at community festivals and pageants dressed as someone else. As Fumiko Takase explains in her study of Thomas Middleton, raucous comedy gave sixteenth-century English audiences voyeuristic opportunities to observe the most intimate, as well as exploitive, of human relationships. Play (especially erotic play) is also the thing to amuse the king: for proof, see King Francis I caught in drag as a hermaphrodite in Raymond Waddington's case study. This is the same king whose death monument we can witness at the royal French burial grounds at the cathedral at Saint-Denis; there lies a stone monument of King Francis I, represented—as became possible in the Renaissance—as a male nude! This book suggests through such examples that playing with gender is an erudite and popular Renaissance pursuit.

Alas, those of us who cannot help but laugh at the gender jokes played on the characters discussed in our essays might consider Sigmund Freud's *Jokes and Their Relation to the Unconscious,* which reminds us of the hostile joke that satirizes and the obscene joke that exposes and the methods of refinement by which jokes of sexual innuendo enter into upper-class society. From the Freudian perspective, which Huizinga announces is not his, even the playfulness of so-called innocent jokes serves to overcome deeply seated inhibitions.[8] The playful, yet intensely serious, ways in which characters in male-authored Renaissance texts cut exceptional women down to size, expose female sexuality, or take their pleasure at women's expense are explored especially in the essays by Nancy Gutierrez, Alison Taufer, Susanne Woods, and Naomi Yavneh.

This Renaissance pastime certainly has moral, social, and political implications for the behavior considered "feminine" or "masculine." Is the evidence of gender play a sign that gender categories are in transition during the period from the fourteenth through the seventeenth centuries? Or does the evidence simply mark another battle in the perennial war between the sexes? Happenings deemed perennial were considered outside the realm of the historical before Lucien Febvre and Marc Bloch, founders of the Annales school, brought attention to their enduring historical importance.

Perhaps soon the list of premodern societal changes on the basis of which many historians have discarded the label "Renaissance" for that of "Age of Transition" will include "gender categories in transition."[9] If so, does the kind of playing with gender detected by our authors indicate a greater degree of freedom in engendering the self, a backlash at those deemed "other," or—as I suspect—a hierarchical, class-based, regionally varied structure of increased opportunities for some and increased repression for others?

On the one hand, the emphasis on androgynous figures who cross the traditional boundary lines of gender may serve as a powerful ideological device for transforming the social construction of gender. In a seminal essay, Joan Kelly argues that Christine de Pizan and Marie de Gournay cite powerful women from the remote past to suggest that the restriction of women's powers is recent and historical.[10] On the other hand, in the age of the Renaissance, when numerous tracts are produced in praise or defamation of woman, dwelling on an "exceptional" woman as "a monstrosity" may serve to reinforce the gender-conforming traits of the numerous "ordinary" or "normal" women.[11] For example, Allison Coudert, drawing on the work of historians of science Lorraine Daston and Katharine Park, has argued that the preoccupation with hermaphrodites in Renaissance medical treatises, as well as in sensational popular works, indicates an anxiety about gender roles that contributes to the increased persecution of witches.[12] Similarly, in Nancy Gutierrez's essay we see Iago's subversive maligning of Desdemona and Othello's gullibility as responses to the "disorder" of Desdemona's defiance of her father and of social mores in her interracial marriage with Othello. Renaissance literary tales of women, like the documents produced by educated Renaissance women, are Janus-like, reflecting optimism in youth and disappointment in maturity, novelty in feminine innovation and continuity in misogynist restriction; nevertheless, the literary and biographical evidence attests to the public importance in the Renaissance of self-conscious gender construction and of women's struggles.

The plays discussed in part I (Shakespeare's *Othello* and Middleton's *A Mad World, My Masters*) exemplify how, in the dualistic framework common to Western thought, the fashioning of the self is inseparably tied to conceptualizing the nonself (for the male, the female; for the God-loving person, the demon-worshiping witch; for the virtuous person, the lush). Yet parts II and III show that the Renaissance outlook transcends simple polarities in its complex symbolism: Renaissance thinkers, influenced by the concept of the "holy," "triangular" number three, often visualize patterns of triads (e.g., male, female, hermaphrodite) or triangular love relationships among characters (e.g., Othello, Iago, and Desdemona).

The triad of mythical original beings described by Aristophanes in Plato's *Symposium* poses a problem to Renaissance systems of classification.

Translated into Latin in the fifteenth century along with the *Republic,* the *Symposium* presents to Renaissance readers the comic description of three original spherical beings, each fully equipped with two heads, two sets of genitalia, four arms, and four legs. Having been disobedient to the Deity, the male sphere is split by the Deity into two males who each seek the other half, the female sphere into female lovers, and the androgyne into heterosexual lovers. Plato's amusing and very descriptive myth of the androgyne adds to the lore about Hermaphroditus and the medical prodigies of hermaphrodites. Ficino's influential commentary on the *Symposium,* in its concern to uphold spiritual love first and heterosexuality as a mere necessity, scorns the homosexual implications of the *Symposium.*[13] Of course, it is hard for anyone (even the Neoplatonist Ficino), no matter how ethereally minded, to attempt to visualize a hermaphrodite and yet miss the joke that in the bodily unity of coitus, the hermaphrodite (two sexes unified) everywhere does in fact, not fiction, populate the world.

Naomi Yavneh's essay focuses not on Ficino but on Leone Ebreo, who reinterprets the *Symposium* in the light of both his Jewish tradition and the then-fashionable Neoplatonism. He enobles heterosexual attraction in the *Dialoghi d'amore,* where the lover and beloved, namely Philo and Sophia, participate in a dialogue procreative of philosophy ("love of wisdom"). The recently documented impact of Leone Ebreo's hermaphroditic model on Cervantes, as well as on Milton, serves to highlight the importance of Yavneh's essay in this volume.[14] In the Renaissance, a flurry of interest in Hebraica among Christian humanists expands Christian awareness that the Talmud views the original human being as both male and female. A correlation, rarely mentioned in this context, is that the conventional Renaissance artistic rendition of God creating Eve from Adam (as on the ceiling of the Sistine Chapel) shows the two in one: a female body from the waist up emerging from a male body.[15] The hermaphrodite thus is not a fringe, marginal issue: derived from several overlapping traditions, he/she is significant in the Renaissance worldview, raising significant philosophical and theological questions on the origin of human nature and on the purpose of physical attraction and love.

This collection of literary and historical essays begins with a major secular literary genre of the Renaissance—the play. With both male and female roles performed by a cast of male actors and tickets sold to men and women from diverse walks of life, the social setting of the English Renaissance theater allows viewers to identify with characters different from themselves, to fashion themselves in new roles.[16] In part I, "Fashioning the Self and the Other," Nancy Gutierrez effectively shows in her analysis of *Othello*[17] how lower-class Iago adopts stereotypical feminine attributes (changeability, cleverness, and a witchlike reliance on verbal formulas, or charms) to refashion Desdemona in the eyes of her husband from a chaste wife to a "witch." Explaining as witchlike behavior what earlier critics had viewed as the Satanic in Iago, and departing from customary interpretations of his manipulative behavior as homosexual or Machiavellian,[18] Gutierrez applies the perspectives of gender studies and psychoanalysis to a discussion of Iago as a conscious actor, a manipulator.[19] Thus she joins Carol T. Neely, Stephen Greenblatt, and other recent critics who view the source of the tragedy to be Iago's and Othello's cultural anxieties about sexuality, women, and marriage. Approaching the play in the historicist framework of the multiple threats to Renaissance English patriarchal order posed by the witch, the adulteress, and the traitorous courtier, Gutierrez refreshingly reassesses the play in the context of the Jacobean fear of witchcraft.[20]

On a lighter note, Fumiko Takase's playful enjoyment in the comic provides an amusing analysis of plot and character in Thomas Middleton's *A Mad World, My Masters,* a comedy about human lust for money and sex. Bawdy and raucous, the characters of the Courtesan and Mistress Harebrain are *exempla* of male-authored female self-fashioning for knavery at its best or worst, as the perspective of the viewer might be.[21]

In the second section, as in the first, we confront many characters of the Renaissance imagination pursuing the gendered "other." In the travel reports and maps of newly discovered lands, woodcuts of Amazons (the "other"—paradoxically barbarian, yet effeminate) confront Renaissance viewers. Interested particularly in that merger of Amazon woman with colonial "other," our case studies of the Spanish *Amadís Cycle* and of Spenser's *Faerie Queene* indicate that encountering, battling, mimicking, and domesticating the Amazon is a significant pursuit of literary geniuses as well as colonial officials. Alison Taufer shows that texts about Amazons in Herodotus, Diodorus Siculus, and Strabo reappear in Renaissance explorers' so-called descriptions of the Amazons they claim to have seen among the Indians. Although *Amadís de Gaule* and its numerous imitations in the various vernaculars have been recognized as very important for the development of the Renaissance romance, the Spanish version by Feliciano de Silva has been relatively neglected in the studies of Renaissance views of the Amazon.[22] In a concrete Spanish-American context, we explore peak moments in de Silva's *Amadís Cycle*—when Amazon queens shed some of their "otherness" and convert to Christianity. The title of part II, "Refashioning Gender: Appropriating the Amazon," highlights the moments in Renaissance literary texts when Amazons marry or convert, moments when the dominant patriarchal hierarchies bring under submission the "other," whether deviant warrior women or differing native peoples.

Feminist interest in Amazons stems from the recognition that reading ancient legends might have broadened the modes of signification open to the Renaissance reader, particularly by extending the discourse on gender to include heroic and autonomous female figures. For example, just as more of us are noticing in viewing Michelangelo's newly cleaned Sistine Chapel ceiling that sibyls take their place amid Old Testament heroes and heroines, so too are we seeing afresh that in Renaissance gender discourse (such as Boccaccio's *De claris mulieribus* or Christine de Pizan's *Livre de la cité des dames*) figures such as Amazons (almost a self-contradiction—a female who is heroic) are conjured up to fill the void of the absent history of women (again a paradox—public words or deeds by those praised for silence). Nonetheless, the feminist reappraisal disappointingly shows that a masculinist bias affects Renaissance rereading of the myths. The integration of the Amazon into European literature reflects codes of repression and subjugation in Renaissance European society,[23] in particular, colonialism in the Americas, the crisis of churches seeking converts overseas while losing souls to dissent in Europe, and the legal, theological, and ideological investment in conceptualizing the adult woman as wife.

Similarly, Susanne Woods's rereading of Spenser's Radigund presents her from a sixteenth-century perspective as representative of Amazons past and present, as "observed" by Sir Walter Ralegh in his *History of the World*. Woods's attention to Spenser's detailed description of Radigund adorning herself in armor for battle gives us a glimpse of the Renaissance fascination with cross-dressing. Woods emphasizes how this scene exemplifies Spenser's mimetic characterization of Radigund as "an imaginative version of a perceived historical reality" (pp. 53–54). Diachronic in her concern to present Spenser from both a twentieth-century perspective and a sixteenth-century one, Woods sympathetically analyzes Radigund as a victim who has little option but to manipulate to find authority in a male world. There is tyranny in both Radigund's use of girlish wiles and her own submission to her passions, as well as in the blame Spenser places on Radigund for the crimes she has endured. Quite consciously, Woods draws readers away from the previous critical attention to allegorical structures in Spenser's *Fairie Queene* (not disputing that in genre theory it is a prime example of allegory) in her skillful study of the Spenserian representation of gendered power relationships.[24]

In a stimulating essay that contributes to the reconstruction of the composition of the *New Arcadia* (the *Arcadia* as revised incompletely by Sir Philip Sidney),[25] Margaret Sullivan focuses on Sidney's struggle with the overlapping hierarchies of gender and class. Following on recent studies of Sidney's political stance vis-à-vis Elizabeth's government,[26] she appropriately expands the presentation of his political theory to include not only macropolitical relationships (ruler and subjects) but also micropolitical relationships (man and dependent wife and daughters). Sullivan portrays Sidney as caught between his vested interest in ensuring that nobility and inheritance may be transmitted matrilineally and his patriarchal concern that female sexuality be under masculine control. Margaret Sullivan links Pyrocles' disguising himself as an Amazon to Sidney's unresolved conflicts concerning gender and class, especially his recognition of the arbitrary nature of the gendered hierarchy of male property rights.[27] In Sullivan's innovative interpretation, that Sidney breaks off his manuscript at the point where Pamela and Philoclea make claims for female autonomy is evidence of his irresolution and discomfort. In revealing Sidney's quandary at the possibility of Amazon behavior as a precedent and role model for independent women, Sullivan joins Woods and Taufer in showing masculine appropriation of the Amazon.

As if the pursuit and taming of Amazons were not exercise enough for the Renaissance imagination, some authors toy with the challenge of imagining and even becoming a hermaphrodite. In part III, "Envisioning the Hermaphrodite," Naomi Yavneh highlights the ways in which Leone Ebreo (Jehudah Abrabenel) radically departs from Ficino's commentary on the *Symposium*. By avoiding any mention of the homoerotic spherical beings in Plato's *Symposium* while affirming only the hermaphroditic sphere, Leone Ebreo interprets Plato's dialogue in a way that accords with his Jewish acceptance of sex, marriage, and procreation as natural and good. The essay contains evidence that Leone contributes to Neoplatonic theory a more positive attitude toward heterosexual lovemaking, while at the same time working within the formative sexist gender constructs of the Western tradition—the Aristotelian model of the female contribution to generation as material and the male contribution as active and seminal (p. 86) and the common medieval analogy of the "masculine" as a symbol for the intellect and the "feminine" as a symbol for the body (pp. 94–95).[28]

Alongside Leone's hermaphroditic Adam stands the "monstrously bisexual Francis I," as Raymond Waddington describes Modena's portrait of Francis I. Breaking with art historical analysis of the work as emblematic[29] and analyzing art in the mode of the journal *Representations*, Waddington argues that Modena's portrait must be understood in the context of such biographical details as Francis's military defeat at Pavia and the amorous pursuits that resulted in his syphilis. The essay links the hermaphroditic portrait to Rosso's drawings at Fountainebleau on the Mars and Venus theme. There, a reticent Francis (Mars) and his amorous new wife, Eleanor (Venus), are mocked by parodies of the god of war with genitals the size of the prepubescent Cupid's and scenes of lesbianism wherein male sexuality is eclipsed. Describing a plethora of connections between the court at Urbino and the court at Fountainebleau, Waddington suggests that Castiglione's *Il Cortegiano* had an important impact on the court at Fountainebleau. In particular, Waddington argues that the Ciceronian discourse on wit delivered by Castiglione's character Bibbiena illuminates the humor of mock praise in the captions to the drawings at Fontainebleau. Most significant for the notion of Renaissance playing with gender is the evidence that Cicero's influential *De oratore* teaches Renaissance readers not only skill in formal oratory but also the way to make an artful Ciceronian joke.[30] Waddington's essay offers new insights into Francis, who was influenced by the tradition of "a laughing or witty ruler" to the unusual point of accepting self-parody as a man-woman. Waddington concludes that Francis was "aware that criticism and satire embraced and diffused into harmless laughter are more endurable than when hidden beneath a facade of facile praise" (p. 125).

The essays in *Playing with Gender: A Renaissance Pursuit* exemplify in style and content the skillful Renaissance art of exploring gendered relationships (and what relationships are not gendered?) with grace and wit. The essential aspects of humanist perceptions of the comic are shown in play, treatise, and image alike: juxtaposition of contraries (e.g., Adam as hermaphrodite, passionate Venus together with limp Mars), incongruity (e.g., pagan female warrior reborn through Christianity or marriage, Othello and Iago as married couple), and sexual behavior exaggerated in *braggadocio* (raucous lust, seductive bewitchment).[31]

In discussing perceptions of the comic in the Renaissance, an age that best articulates the paradox of the wisdom of the fool,[32] let us pause a moment to reconsider Erasmus's persona Folly: "I hope that sex [female] is not so foolish as to take offense at this, that I myself, being a woman, and folly too, have attributed folly to them."[33] As participants in the feminist rhetoric of outrage at the misogynist statements and images found in Renaissance literature, treatise, pamphlet, and picture,[34] might our generation not be Folly herself speaking out against Folly? Alas, to look from another angle at our "serious" work of undermining patriarchal culture, might we recognize that two decades ago a smile strike[35] initiated the somber age of the feminist literary critic? Might it be possible that, matured into the Erasmian figure of Folly, she now takes Epicurean delight in smiling once again with the Amazons, adulteresses, witches, and hermaphrodites who people the world of the Renaissance imagination?[36]

NOTES

My appreciation extends to editors Allison Coudert and Jean Brink for their thoughtful readings of earlier drafts of this introduction. To hypothesize in unison that playing with gender is a major Renaissance trait raises rather than settles the issue of how to interpret the phenomenon. This interpretation—buoyant in enthusiasm for Renaissance explorations of human diversity and individuality, skeptical and liberal in its posing of a multiplicity of possible historical and feminist approaches, and hopeful in giving the last word to Folly—is strictly my own.

1. Stephen Greenblatt, *Renaissance Self-fashioning: From More to Shakespeare* (Chicago: University of Chicago Press, 1980). The implications of the fashioning of self and "other" for Renaissance gender concepts are explored in Stephen Greenblatt, "Fiction and Friction," *Shakespearian Negotiations* (Berkeley: University of California Press, 1988), 66–93, and in Marjorie Garber, ed., *Cannibals, Witches, and Divorce: Estranging the Renaissance* (Baltimore: Johns Hopkins University Press, 1987).

2. Simone de Beauvoir, *The Second Sex,* trans. and ed. H. M. Parshley (New York: Alfred A. Knopf, 1978), "Introduction", xvi–xxiii, xxix; Tzvetan Todorov, *The Conquest of America: The Question of the Other,* trans. Richard Howard (New York: Harper & Row, 1984).

3. Simon Shephard, *Amazons and Warrior Women: Varieties of Feminism in Seventeenth-Century Drama* (New York: St. Martin's Press, 1981); Page duBois, *Centaurs and Amazons: Women and the Pre-History of the Great Chain of Being* (Ann Arbor: University of Michigan Press, 1982); Abby W. Kleinbaum, *The War against the Amazons* (New York: McGraw-Hill, 1983); Wm. Blake Tyrrell, *Amazons: A Study in Athenian Mythmaking* (Baltimore: Johns Hopkins University Press, 1984); Olive Patricia Dickason, *The Myth of the Savage: And the Beginnings of French Colonialism in the Americas* (Edmonton: University of Alberta Press, 1984). On "warrior woman" among the Spanish, see Mary Elizabeth Perry, "The Manly Woman: A Historical Case Study," in *New Gender Scholarship: Breaking Old Boundaries* (special issue of *American Behavioral Scientist*), ed. Harry Brod and Walter Williams (Beverly Hills, Cal.: Sage, 1987), and *"La monja alférez:* Myth, Gender, and Manly Woman in a Spanish Renaissance Drama," *LA CHISPA* 8 (1988): 239–49. On male actors playing male characters in Amazon disguise, see Winfried Schleiner, "Male Cross-Dressing and Transvestism in Renaissance Romances," *The Sixteenth Century Journal* 19 (1988): 605–19.

4. Marie Delcourt, *Hermaphrodite: Mythes et rites de la bisexualité dans l'antiquité classique* (Paris: P.G.F., 1958); Mircea Éliade, *Mephistopheles and the Androgyne,* trans. J. M. Cohen (New York: Sheed and Ward, 1965); Edgar Wind, *Pagan Mysteries in the Renaissance* (New York: W. W. Norton & Company, 1968), 200, 211–17; Lauren Silberman, "Mythographic Transformations of Ovid's Hermaphrodite," *The Sixteenth Century Journal* 19 (1988): 643–52. See also Stevie Davies, *The Feminine Reclaimed: The Idea of Woman in Spenser, Shakespeare, and Milton* (Lexington: University Press of Kentucky, 1986), which from a Jungian perspective interprets the Renaissance ideal as a Platonic-Hermetist longing for unity in the androgyne or hermaphrodite. For Milton specifically, see Diane Kelsey McColley, *Milton's Eve* (Urbana: University of Illinois Press, 1983); and Julia M. Walker, ed., *Milton and the Idea of Woman* (Urbana: University of Illinois Press, 1988).

5. For "gender" as a category in literary analysis, see overviews in Elaine Showalter, *Speaking of Gender* (New York: Routledge, 1989), 1–13; Gayle Greene and Coppélia Kahn, eds., *Making a Difference: Feminist Literary Criticism* (London: Methuen, 1985) "Introduction"; and from another perspective, K. Ruthven, *Feminist Literary Studies*

(Cambridge: Cambridge University Press, 1984). For "gender" as an analytic tool in historical study, see Joan Wallech Scott, "Gender: A Useful Category of Historical Analysis," *Gender and the Politics of History* (New York: Columbia University Press, 1988), especially pp. 42–44. Applications of gender studies to Renaissance studies include James M. Saslow, *Ganymede in the Renaissance: Homosexuality in Art and Society* (New Haven: Yale University Press, 1986), especially pp. 10–16, 75–84; and " 'A Veil of Ice between My Heart and the Fire': Michelangelo's Sexual Identity and Early Modern Constructs of Homosexuality," *Genders* 2 (1988): 77–90. An excellent set of collected essays is Margaret W. Ferguson, Maureen Quilligan, and Nancy J. Vickers, eds., *Rewriting the Renaissance: The Discourses of Sexual Difference in Early Modern Europe* (Chicago: University of Chicago Press, 1986). The homoerotic in the Renaissance is also discussed in Judith C. Brown, *Immodest Acts* (New York: Oxford University Press, 1986); John Boswell, *Christianity, Social Tolerance, and Homosexuality* (Chicago: University of Chicago Press, 1980); Alan Bray, *Homosexuality in Renaissance England* (London: Gay Men's Press, 1982); and Ken Gerard and Gert Kekma, eds., *The Pursuit of Sodomy* (New York: Harrington, 1988).

6. If proof is needed of Renaissance scientific and erotic fascination with hermaphrodites, enjoy the many Renaissance "artistic" renderings of hermaphrodites in Elémire Zolla, *The Androgyne: Reconciliation of Male and Female* (New York: Crossroad, 1981). See also M. C. Horowitz, "The 'Science' of Embryology before the Discovery of the Ovum," in *Connecting Spheres: Women in the Western World, 1550–1980*, ed. M. Boxer and J. Quattaert (New York: Oxford University Press, 1987). On the fears that gender transformation might lead to sex transformation, see Katharine Eisaman Maus, "Playhouse Flesh and Blood: Sexual Ideology and the Restoration," *English Literary History* 46 (1979): 595–617; Laura Levine, "Men in Women's Clothing: Antitheatricality and Effeminization from 1579 to 1642," *Criticism* 28 (1986): 121–45; and Greenblatt, *Shakespearian Negotiations*, 66–93. For an example of humor counteracting erudite superstition in the late sixteenth century, see M. C. Horowitz, "Montaigne versus Bodin on Ancient Tales of Demonology," *Proceedings of the Western Society of French History* 16 (1989): 103–10.

7. J. Huizinga, *Homo Ludens: A Study of the Play-Element in Culture* (New York: Roy Publishers, 1950), "Foreward." For a recent approach to *homo ludens*, see Natalie Zemon Davis's historical-anthropological studies of topsy-turvy play, women on top, carnival, masks, misrule, and gendered role play in *Society and Culture in Early Modern France* (Stanford: Stanford University Press, 1975), especially pp. 97–189; her study of Bertrande de Rols (appearing as faithful wife while adulteress) in *The Return of Martin Guerre* (Cambridge: Harvard University Press, 1983), especially pp. 27–35, 43–51, 68–72; and her study of the gendered rhetoric necessary for successful legal appeal in *Fiction in the Archives: Pardon Tales and Their Tellers in Sixteenth-Century France* (Stanford: Stanford University Press, 1987).

8. Sigmund Freud, *The Standard Edition of the Complete Psychological Works*, 24 vols., trans. and ed. James Strachey (London: Hogarth Press, 1966–73) 8: 97, 100, 132, 138. His comments are scarce on specifically female-authored jokes. For Freud's critical discussion of the myth in relationship to narcissism and an instinct for reunification, see his *Beyond the Pleasure Principle*, in *The Standard Edition*, 18: 57–58.

9. See the journal *Annales: Économies, sociétés, civilisations.* See also Wallace Ferguson, *The Renaissance in Historical Thought: Five Centuries of Interpretations* (Boston: Houghton Mifflin, 1948) and *Europe in Transition, 1300–1520* (Boston: Houghton Mifflin, 1962). For one of the first explorations of the questions posed here, see Joan Kelly, *Women, History, and Theory* (Chicago: University of Chicago Press, 1984). "Renaming the Renaissance" was the theme of the Renaissance Society of America National Conference at Harvard University, March 1989. The plenary session on economics and urban development supported the concept of an age of transition.

10. See "Early Feminist Theory and the 'Querelle des Femmes,'" in Kelly, *Women, History, and Theory,* especially p. 84. There is growing attention to the discrepancies between men's and women's readings, as in the way Christine de Pizan reads the ancient mythological figures differently from Boccaccio. See, e.g., Valerie Wayne, "Zenobia in Medieval and Renaissance Literature," in *Ambiguous Realities: Women in the Middle Ages and Renaissance,* ed. Carole Levin (Detroit: Wayne State University Press, 1987), 54–57; and Susan Groag Bell, "Christine de Pizan (1364–1430): Humanism and the Problem of a Studious Woman," *Feminist Studies* 3 (1975): 176–80. Seeking precedents and models is one source for the continuing fascination among feminist critics in prehistorical "matriarchies" and in androgynous figures such as those discussed in this volume. As an example of the continuing creative impact of ancient myth, let us sample one contemporary discipline—psychology: see the humanistic June Singer, *Androgyny: Toward a New Theory of Sexuality* (Garden City, N.Y.: Anchor, 1976), 1–3; and the social scientific Ellen Piel Cook, *Psychological Androgyny* (New York: Pergamon Press, 1985).

11. Frances Lee Utley, *The Crooked Rib: An Analytical Index to the Argument about Women* (New York: Octagon Books, 1970); Linda Woodbridge, *Women and the English Renaissance: Literature and the Nature of Womankind, 1540–1620* (Urbana: University of Illinois Press, 1984); M. C. Horowitz, "The 'Woman Question' in Renaissance Texts," *History of European Ideas* 8 (1987): 587–95. In calling female humanists "Amazons," male humanists link female learning with aggression and cause female self-doubts about becoming desexed, neither male nor female. The most psychologically perceptive studies are Margaret King, "Book-lined Cells: Women and Humanism in the Early Italian Renaissance," in *Beyond Their Sex,* ed. Patricia H. Labalme (New York: New York University Press, 1984), 79–90; and Anthony Grafton and Lisa Jardine, "Women Humanists: Education for What?" *From Humanism to the Humanities: Education and Liberal Arts in Fifteenth- and Sixteenth-Century Europe* (Cambridge: Harvard University Press, 1986), 29–58. For a sampling of current biographies of Renaissance women who faced the problems inherent in fashioning an identity as an educated woman, see Jean R. Brink, ed., *Female Scholars: A Tradition of Learned Women before 1800* (Montreal: Eden Press, 1980); and Katharina Wilson, ed., *Women Writers of the Renaissance and Reformation* (Athens: University of Georgia Press, 1987).

12. Allison Coudert, "The Myth of the Improved Status of Protestant Women: The Case of the Witchcraze," in *Politics of Gender in Early Modern Europe,* ed. J. R. Brink, A. Coudert, and M. C. Horowitz (Kirksville, Mo.: Sixteenth Century Journal Publishers, 1989), citing Lorraine Daston and Katharine Park, "Hermaphrodites in

Renaissance France," *Critical Matrix* 1 (1985). Also see Daston and Park, "Unnatural Conceptions: The Study of Monsters in Sixteenth-Century France and England," *Past and Present* 92 (1981): 20–54.

13. Marsilio Ficino, *Commentary on Plato's Symposium on Love,* trans. Sears Jayne (Dallas: Spring Publications, 1985), 135.

14. Diane Wilson, "Cervantes's *Labors of Persiles:* Working (in) the In-Between," *Literary Theory/Literary Texts,* ed. Patricia Parker and David Quint (Baltimore: Johns Hopkins University Press, 1986), 150–82. See also works on Milton, note 4.

15. M. C. Horowitz, "The Image of God in Man—Is Woman Included?" *Harvard Theological Review* 72 (1979): 175–206. Illustrations in Zolla, *The Androgyne,* pp. 38, 41, and in the Princeton Index of Christian Art, s.v. "Adam and Eve."

16. For an alternative Renaissance theatrical context wherein females play all the roles, see Elissa Weaver, "Spiritual Fun: A Study of Sixteenth-Century Tuscan Convent Theater," *Women in the Middle Ages and the Renaissance,* ed. Mary Beth Rose (Syracuse: Syracuse University Press, 1986).

17. Scholarship on *Othello* is extensive; see John Hazel Smith, *Shakespeare's "Othello": A Bibliography* (New York: AMS Press, 1988). For a sample of recent interpretations, see Joan Wain, ed., *Shakespeare—"Othello": A Casebook* (London: Macmillan, 1985); and Peter Davison, *"Othello": The Critics Debate* (London: Macmillan, 1988).

18. For a brief overview of these three schools of interpreting Iago's motivation, see Stanley E. Hyman, *Iago: Some Approaches to the Illusion of His Motivation* (New York: Atheneum, 1970). For an analysis of recent theatrical performances, see Martin L. Wine, *"Othello": Text and Performance* (London: Macmillan, 1984).

19. For a sampling in Shakespeare scholarship of diverse critical approaches on gender, see Carolyn Ruth Swift Lenz, Gayle Greene, and Carol Thomas Neely, eds., *The Woman's Part: Feminist Criticism of Shakespeare* (Urbana: University of Illinois Press, 1980), with an *Othello* bibliography on pp. 329–30; and Patricia Parker and Geoffrey Hartman, eds., *Shakespeare and the Question of Theory* (New York: Methuen, 1985), especially Parker's essay on *Othello,* pp. 54–75. Psychoanalytic approaches may be found in Murray M. Schwartz and Coppélia Kahn, eds., *Representing Shakespeare: New Psychoanalytic Essays* (Baltimore: Johns Hopkins University Press, 1980), with a bibliography on pp. 264–88; *Shakespeare Survey* 40 (1987): 190–92. See also the special issue on feminist criticism of *Shakespeare Quarterly* 38, no. 1 (1987).

20. Carol Thomas Neely, "Women and Men in *Othello,*" and Stephen Greenblatt, "The Improvisation of Power," in *William Shakespeare's "Othello": Modern Critical Interpretations,* ed. Harold Bloom (New York: Chelsea House, 1987), especially pp. 37–41, 80–81. Gutierrez adds another chapter to the study of cultural anxieties explored in Lisa Jardine, *Still Harping on Daughters: Women and Drama in the Age of Shakespeare* (Totowa, N.J.: Barnes & Noble Books, 1983), and to the study of the changing sexual discourses of the English Renaissance in the parallel public and private realms discussed in Mary Beth Rose, *The Expense of Spirit: Love and Sexuality in English Renaissance* (Ithaca: Cornell University Press, 1988).

21. Related work includes Stephen Hannaford, " 'My Money Is My Daughter':

Sexual and Financial Possession in English Renaissance Comedy," *Jahrbuch der Deutschen Shakespeare-Gesellschaft West* (Heidelberg: Quelle & Meyer, 1984): 93–110; Kenneth Friedenrich, ed., *Essays Celebrating Thomas Middleton, 1580–1980* (New York: AMS, 1983); and Ania Loomba, *Race, Gender, Renaissance Drama* (New York: St. Martin's Press, 1989).

22. See note 3.

23. This historicist perspective has parallels in Stephen Greenblatt, ed., *The Power of Forms in the English Renaissance* (Norman: University of Oklahoma Press, 1982), and *Renaissance Self-fashioning;* Louis Adrian Montrose, "Shaping Fantasies: Figurations of Gender and Power in Elizabethan Culture," *Representations* 2 (1983): 61–94; David Quint, *Literary Theory/Literary Texts*, "Introduction," i–vi; and Arthur F. Kinney and Dan S. Collins, eds., *Renaissance Historicism: Selections from "English Literary Renaissance"* (Amherst: University of Massachusetts Press, 1988).

24. Allegorical interpretations are defended against historicist ones in T. K. Dunseath, *Spenser's Allegory of Justice in Book Five of "The Faerie Queene"* (Princeton: Princeton University Press, 1968). For a survey see Foster Provost, "Treatments of Theme and Allegory in Twentieth-Century Criticism of *The Faerie Queene"* and Bernard Vondersmith, "A Bibliography of Criticism of *The Faerie Queene,* 1900–1970," in *Contemporary Thought on Spenser,* ed. Richard C. Frushell and Bernard J. Vondersmith (Carbondale: Southern Illinois University Press, 1975). A prominent example of the deconstructivist rejection of "reducing Spenser's text to one-to-one allegorical meanings" and interest in studying disequilibrium is Jonathan Goldberg's *Endlesse Work: Spenser and the Structures of Discourse* (Baltimore: Johns Hopkins University Press, 1981). For views of Spenser among his earliest readers, see R. M. Cummings, *Spenser: The Critical Heritage* (London: Routledge & Kegan Paul, 1971).

25. For a sampling of Sidney scholarship, see Arthur F. Kinney, ed., *Essential Articles for the Study of Sir Philip Sidney* (Hamden, Conn.: Shoe String, 1986), with annotated bibliography on pp. 443–58; Gary F. Waller and Michael D. Moore, eds., *Sir Philip Sidney and the Interpretation of Renaissance Culture* (London: Croom-Helm, 1984). On the evidence of Sidney's own revision of the texts, see Sir Philip Sidney, *The Countess of Pembroke's Arcadia (The New Arcadia),* ed. Victor Skretkowicz (Oxford: Clarendon Press, 1987); and William Godshalk, "Sidney's Revision of the *Arcadia* Books III–VII" and Annabel M. Patterson, " 'Under . . . Pretty Tales': Intention in Sidney's *Arcadia,* " in Kinney, ed., *Essential Articles for the Study of Sir Philip Sidney,* pp. 311–12, 357–58. Coburn Freer differs from current Sidney scholarship in the literary role she attributes to the Countess of Pembroke; see Freer, "Mary Sidney: Countess of Pembroke," in Wilson, ed., *Women Writers of the Renaissance and Reformation.*

26. Richard C. McCoy, *Sir Philip Sidney: Rebellion in Arcadia* (New Brunswick: Rutgers University Press, 1979); and Martin N. Raitiere, *Faire Bitts: Sir Philip Sidney and Renaissance Political Theory* (Pittsburgh: Duquesne University Press, 1984).

27. Recent social histories researching the impact of class and gender distinctions in Renaissance England include Susan Dwyer Amussen, *An Ordered Society: Gender and Class in Early Modern England* (New York: Basil Blackwell, 1988); and Martin Ingram, *Church Courts, Sex, and Marriage in England, 1570–1640* (Cambridge: Cambridge University Press, 1987).

28. M. C. Horowitz, "Aristotle and Woman," *Journal of the History of Biology* 9, no. 2 (1976): 183–213.

29. On parallel research on Rabelais's hermaphrodite, see Carla Freccero, "The Other and the Same: The Image of the Hermaphrodite in Rabelais," in Ferguson et al., eds., *Rewriting the Renaissance.* On awareness at the court of Elizabeth I of Francis I's royal use of the hermaphrodite, see Leah S. Marcus, "Shakespeare's Comic Heroines, Elizabeth I, and the Political Uses of Androgyny," in Rose, ed., *Women in the Middle Ages and the Renaissance.*

30. Grafton and Jardine, *From Humanism to the Humanities,* "Conclusion," especially p. 218. Paula Findlen's recent article "Jokes of Nature and Jokes of Knowledge: The Playfulness of Scientific Discourse in Early Modern Europe" explores parallel forms of playfulness. *Renaissance Quarterly,* 43, no. 2 (1990): 292–331.

31. David Farley-Hills, *The Comic in Renaissance Comedy* (Totowa, N.J.: Barnes & Noble, 1981), chap. 1.

32. Walter Kaiser, s.v. "Wisdom of the Fool," *Dictionary of the History of Ideas,* 5 vols., ed. Philip P. Wiener (New York: Charles Scribner's Sons, 1973), 4: 515–21. For recent affirmation of the impact of Erasmus's *Encomium moriae* on Tudor humanist poetics, especially on wordplay, Janus-like figures or two-sided remarks, impersonation of a historical individual, and feigning a person who is fictional, see Arthur F. Kinney, *Humanist Poetics: Thought, Rhetoric, and Fiction in Sixteenth-Century England* (Amherst: University of Massachusetts Press, 1986), especially pp. 16–17, 35, 41–56, 232, 238, 250.

33. Desiderius Erasmus, *The Praise of Folly* (1668), trans. John Wilson (Ann Arbor: University of Michigan Press, 1971), 27.

34. For example, Brink et al., eds., *Politics of Gender in Early Modern Europe.*

35. Betty Friedan, *The Feminine Mystique* (New York: W. W. Norton & Company, 1963). In chapter 2, "The Happy Housewife Heroine," she states: "I wonder if a few problems are not somewhat better than this smiling empty passivity" (p. 64).

36. For Renaissance precedents for making the misogynist the butt of the joke, note the titles *The Women's Sharpe Revenge* (1640) and *Ester Hath Hang'd Haman* (1617).

Playing with Gender

PART I

Fashioning the Self and the Other

Witchcraft and Adultery in *Othello:* Strategies of Subversion

NANCY GUTIERREZ

In *Othello,* a female character is believed to have committed adultery, and all three main characters, at one point or another, are accused of witchcraft. Given that both activities were considered "female" crimes in Renaissance England and that both were considered subversive—in an adulterous relationship, the woman rebels against her husband, and in a witch's pact, the witch renounces the true God—their close association is logical. Further, both activities are marked by sexual betrayal, for in adultery a woman sleeps with a man not her husband, and in witchcraft the devil binds a witch to himself through sexual intercourse. In this essay, I focus on witchcraft in *Othello* as a model of erotic configurations and character relationships, a locus of power available to both the dominant and the marginalized in the play. In act I, the dominant power group, in the person of Brabantio, uses witchcraft to define and thus contain the personally and socially disruptive crime of adultery: Brabantio believes Othello enchanted Desdemona into betraying her father, her class, her country, and her race; the threat to order comes from outside the Venetian culture. Iago, a discontented and dissatisfied office seeker, recognizing in Brabantio's accusation of witchcraft a kind of cultural rationalization of the dominant group's own lack of control, destroys Othello by exploiting this same vulnerability. However, his own adoption of "feminine" behavior, as he appropriates "wifely" attitudes and practices witchcraft activities, demonstrates the fluidity of gender boundaries in a culture (Venetian or Elizabethan) that is self-defined as patriarchal.[1]

· · ·

When Brabantio realizes that Desdemona is missing and has probably married Othello, he immediately blames Othello's "witchcraft" for what he perceives as his daughter's uncharacteristic behavior: "Is there not charms / By which the property of youth and maidhood / May be abus'd?" (I.i.171–73),[2] he asks Roderigo. In the next scene Brabantio accuses Othello of having "[enchanted] her" (I.ii.63), of "[practicing] on her with foul charms / [Abusing] her delicate youth with drugs or minerals / That weakens motion" (I.ii.73–75).

3

Othello must be "an abuser of the world, a practicer / Of arts inhibited" (I.ii.78–79). The reason for such accusations, of course, is that Othello is an entirely inappropriate husband for Desdemona: he is not of her world, being a rather rough soldier, used to battle and war, whereas she is a civilized urbanite, used to social niceties and courtesy; he is at least middle-aged, whereas she is a virgin of marriageable age; and finally, he is an alien to her country, a black Moor, and she is a fair and beautiful daughter of one of the city's prominent citizens. To paraphrase Brabantio (and Othello himself, in III.iii.227), nature could not so greatly err unless witchcraft were to blame.

What Brabantio means by witchcraft is considerably more complicated than our modern understanding of the term. Although we certainly are able to grasp the metaphor that Shakespeare creates, we cannot so easily discern the cultural ethos of witchcraft that he presupposes. The witchcraft hysteria of early modern Europe is a complicated phenomenon, one that focuses many tensions of the age, and Shakespeare's play is part and parcel of this cultural anxiety.

The primary characteristic of witchcraft, as it is described in witchcraft treatises and published accounts of witchcraft trials, is that it challenges God's rightful authority.[3] It is a human activity, encouraged, if not initiated, by the devil, that aims to thwart God: "plaine *vsurpation* of the *diuine office*, and a flat peruersion & disgracing of the *diuine* Provide[n]ce," as Thomas Cooper describes it in *The Mystery of Witchcraft*, published in 1617.[4] The motivation for such subversion is the desire for power. Thus, those people who are most likely to become witches are those who are poor and powerless.[5] Women are especially susceptible to witchcraft, because they are "vsually more *ambitious* and *desirous of Soueraignety*, the rather because they are bound to subiection."[6] In other words, because women are marginalized by the patriarchal system, they can be easily tempted to work against it. In fact, any disfranchised, powerless group within a given society might be so tempted. The specific harm that a witch does to another human being is called *maleficium*, that is, any "positive [act] of hostility to the community,"[7] and so it is interpreted by the three Acts of Parliament that made witchcraft a statutory offense in England (1542, 1563, and 1604). Thus, witchcraft is not simply subversive thinking but rather *activity* that disrupts the social order, that is, the status quo as determined by masculine authority.

Given this historical construct, Brabantio's accusation that Othello has bewitched his daughter can be seen as the normal reaction of the dominant power group toward a threat to its authority. Because a woman was the possession of her father before she was given to her husband, Desdemona's clandestine marriage to Othello is, from Brabantio's point of view, a violent and unnatural breach of the normal relationship between father and daughter. Brabantio had thought that Desdemona was naturally submissive and obedient: "A maiden, never bold; / Of spirit so still and quiet that her motion / Blush'd at herself" (I.iii.94–96). As a woman who complies with patriarchal dominance and accepts the status quo, she would be directed by her father in her choice of a husband. Therefore, according to her father, she cannot be the instigator of the break in the father-daughter dyad. The disrupter must be Othello, the outsider. By labeling Othello a witch, Brabantio endows him with the evil power of a demon lover: a devilish spirit who forces himself sexually on a human lover to create more witches, more threats to the established order. In this construct, Othello becomes a representative of every kind of evil, a profound danger to the entire community of Venice. Brabantio, in seeing his world threatened, thus identifies the threat as coming from the outside, a danger that, although real and clearly serious, is nevertheless external, leaving the structures of family and society whole and strong.

The real situation, of course, is that the source of destruction in Brabantio's life is his daughter, not some alien outsider: the disrupter of order comes from within, not from without. The threat to the status quo is all the more serious because the system itself has produced its own enemy. Hence, Brabantio's words to Othello at the end of the trial scene are more than merely querulous and vengeful; they are chillingly true: "She has deceiv'd her father, and may thee" (I.iii.293). If Desdemona can deny her social and political culture by betraying her father, what is to prevent her from disrupting her marriage with Othello? She has subverted the patriarchal system once, she can do it again.

Thus, the first act of the play, which enacts the tragic action in miniature, but with a happy ending for Othello and Desdemona, is more than a demonstration that the civilized world of Venice can control disruptive behavior with its social and political institutions, a conventional interpretation.[8] It also reveals to Iago the crack in the Venetian power structure: woman. When Desdemona rebels against her father and asserts her own will, she does so by placing in priority a woman's right to marry a man of her own choosing, not her subservience to her father's direction. As Lynda E. Boose and Diane Elizabeth Dreher point out in their separate discussions of the play, this very necessary and inevitable transfer of allegiance is nevertheless traumatic for a father who resists his daughter's growth into a mature, adult woman.[9] Therefore, even though women serve as the medium of exchange in a patriarchal society, the means by which men exercise power, part of the very foundation and life of the patriarchal system ironically rests on a kind of female betrayal, when a daughter transfers her allegiance from her father to her husband.[10]

• • •

In a very real sense, Desdemona's marriage to Othello constitutes a kind of adultery with regard to Brabantio and Venetian culture. In Renaissance marriage manuals, adultery is defined as a violation of the marriage contract, "a destruction . . . , a wylfull truce breakynge & periury."[11] Adultery always presupposes another "authority" to whom the woman turns, thus creating a triangular configuration of husband-wife-lover; equally important, if not more so, it includes sexual betrayal as well as rebellion against authority, so that both masculine power and masculine identity are threatened. In her elopement, Desdemona not only rebels against her father's authority but also implicitly acknowledges that she is flouting her father's probable choice of husband (that is, sexual partner) to satisfy her own emotional and physical needs: sexual innuendo colors her disobedience, not only in Iago's coarse humor in act I, scene i, but also in her own and Othello's responses to her living arrangements during the Turkish crisis (I.iii.229–78).

In her rejection of her father and of Venetian values, Desdemona's choice of Othello offers a paradigm of adultery important to the rest of the action of the play.[12] Iago, who feels himself disfranchised because Othello has passed him over for the lieutenantship, creates a lie in which Desdemona is once again in an adulterous triangle. Because Othello has been transformed from alien to insider in the move from Venice to Cyprus, he is, in effect, now the representative of the patriarchy. Consequently, the Moor picks up where Brabantio left off, interpreting Desdemona's betrayal as an attack from without: she, not Cassio, is the rebel and destroyer, and thus she, not Cassio, is the demon lover, the alien tempter whose allegiance is to a different and antagonistic world.[13] But this view of Desdemona is the fabrication of Iago, himself a kind of demon lover intruding on the marriage of Othello and Desdemona. The demonic nature of Iago, controlling and manipulating his world through appropriation of female powers, provides a window onto the cultural intersection of female adultery and witchcraft and, at the same time, calls into question the functional aspect of gender in relationships between men. Both these ideas must be examined more fully.

• • •

The male characters perceive Desdemona to be an ideal woman—chaste, silent, and obedient. According to her father, Desdemona has been "A maiden, never bold; / Of spirit so still and quiet that her motion / Blush'd at herself" (I.iii.94–96). Cassio, in responding to Iago's bawdy sneers, describes Desdemona as "a most exquisite lady," "a most fresh and delicate creature," who has "an inviting" yet "right modest eye," and who "is indeed perfection" (II.iii.18, 20–21, 24–25, 28). But Desdemona's actions in the early part of the play clearly demonstrate that she is neither the submissive and docile daughter Brabantio thinks she is nor the sexually disinterested and virginal woman Cassio pictures. Thus it is easy to dismantle this picture, which is not true in the first place, fashioning in its place its opposite—the image of the woman as whore. And this is exactly what Iago does.

When Iago suggests to Othello that Desdemona might be unfaithful, he very deliberately places her misbehavior in the context of her "unnatural" love for Othello that has caused her to betray her father. He also emphasizes the "deceit" that Desdemona must have practiced against Brabantio in order for Othello to have been successful in his wooing, for both Desdemona and Othello clearly kept their courtship secret, a lack of openness that violates "honesty." Iago says, "She that so young could give out such seeming / To seel her father's eyes up, close as oak, / He thought 'twas witchcraft—" (III.iii.209–11). Iago's words omit Othello's role, thus emphasizing Desdemona's. Further, Iago here deliberately fails to complete his thought so that Othello will naturally come to the logical conclusion the words suggest: that Desdemona used witchcraft on Othello in causing him to love her.

In this famous temptation scene, Iago paints the same picture of Desdemona for Othello that he had for Roderigo: she is "a super-subtle Venetian" who "must change for youth," and who, "when she is sated with [Othello's] body, . . . will find the error of her choice" and "must have change, . . . must" (I.iii.356, 349–52). In reading Desdemona in this way, Iago effectively "deconstructs" her, establishing her for Othello as "the dangerous, supplemental, figural term" that threatens "the stable, literal one."[14] For man, who constitutes himself as the norm, woman is inconstant, metamorphic, and ultimately unknowable.

That Othello is ready to believe Iago we know from the subliminal message in the grammar of the following passage:

> 'Tis not to make me jealous
> To say my wife is fair, feeds well, loves company,
> Is free of speech, sings, plays, and dances well;
> Where virtue is, these are more virtuous. (III.iii.183–86)

Although Othello is apparently denying his proclivity to jealousy and approving of his wife's high spirits, the conditionality in the last line reveals his fundamental insecurity about Desdemona, the inability of ever piercing through appearances. Three hundred lines later Othello responds to Iago's deconstructive reading of Desdemona in a manner congruent with this earlier speech: recognizing her as "other," he labels her "devil" (III.iii.479; III.iv.42; IV.i.43, 240, and 244), thus combining her sexual betrayal with demonic powers and identifying her as that demon lover who tempts

7

human beings to adopt an alien world by overturning their own. As part of the dominant power structure—he identifies himself as one of those "great ones" (III.iii.273)—he envisions the threat to both his private and his public selves as originating in an alien other, just as Brabantio had: "O curse of marriage!" he cries, "That we can call these delicate creatures ours, / And not their appetites" (III.iii.268–70). A woman's appetite, culturally defined as voracious and bestial, is distinct, "other," opposite to the characteristically masculine quality of reason. (And in this play, reason is associated with Venice and its legal and political institutions, the culture Othello has adopted.)

Not only is his conceptualization of an unfaithful Desdemona that of a witch, but Othello's immediate desire to inflict some kind of physical torture on his wife also demonstrates a parallel between the crimes of adultery and witchcraft. Othello threatens to do Desdemona violence, particularly the kind of violence that mutilates or disfigures. For example, late in the temptation scene, he lists several kinds of torture that husbands have been known to practice on their adulterous wives: "cords, or knives, / Poison, or fire, or suffocating streams" (III.iii.388–89).[15] Several lines later he threatens to "tear [Desdemona] all to pieces" (III.iii.431), a threat he repeats later (IV.i.200). Othello's desire to disfigure the woman who he thinks has bewitched and betrayed him suggests a contemporary cultural response to witches, a so-called remedy for a witch's victims termed "scratching." This consists of scratching a witch's face, drawing blood "above the breath," in order to break the spell that the witch has cast, "that so her spirite may haue no power."[16] When Othello threatens Desdemona with mutilation or fragmentation, he too is seeking to take away power, the power of temptation that a woman's beauty has for men.

The similarity of Othello's response to this kind of socially acceptable mutilation of a woman suggests that we may understand the Elizabethan conception of adultery as a cultural equivalent for witchcraft: in both activities, a woman's body becomes the battleground for cultural phobias.[17] Certainly, in documents of the time, both crimes are described in metaphors of the other. A passage from George Gifford's *Discourse of the subtill Practises of Deuilles by VVitches and Sorcerers* is particularly representative of this kind of discourse:

> God saith here [in Leviticus 20:6] that such persons as seeke vnto Coniurers and Witches, doe goe a whoring after deuilles. The soule of man should be kept pure and chast vnto God as a wife vnto her only husband. They should not commit spirituall whoredome with deuilles, as the Lord doth here charge those which seeke vnto deuilles. What a foule thing is this, that such as haue made a solemne vowe in baptisme, to forsake the deuill and all his workes, should now seeke vnto deuilles for help: Hee that committeth

8

adulterie in the flesh, is not to bee suffred. Then how much more are these worthie to bee rooted out, which haue so vnfaithfully broken their vowe made vnto God, and haue committed whoredome with deuills.[18]

Gifford bases his metaphor of sexual betrayal for the crime of witchcraft on the subversive element in both. This language is common to witchcraft manuals and accounts of witchcraft trials of the period; likewise, marriage manuals, religious treatises, legal handbooks, and other didactic writings describe adultery as a kind of witchcraft. The cultural equation of these two female crimes consequently illuminates Shakespeare's own interplay of them in Othello's response to the adultery he believes Desdemona has practiced. Shakespeare's depiction of Iago further demonstrates the nature of power relations that such equivalence suggests.

•   •   •

That apparent docility and contentment hide murderous hatred and rancor is the atavistic fear the patriarchy holds of women, and it is this basic fear that Iago comprehends in his observation of the events of act I. There is no adultery in the play, and no woman practices witchcraft. But so embedded in the male psyche is the fear of such female betrayal that Iago, by himself adopting what the culture identified specifically as female behavior, deludes Othello into believing that Desdemona has used both kinds of female subversion against him.

The extremity of Iago's actions against Othello has fascinated literary scholars and drawn forth a variety of interpretations. Certain critics identify him as a particular kind of social or psychological deviant. For example, Fred West sees him as a psychopath, Martin Wangh identifies him as a homosexual, and Gordon Ross Smith as a paranoiac.[19] Other psychoanalytic critics see him as some part of Othello's psyche.[20] Shakespeare's age seems to have its own suggestion in Francis Bacon's description of the envious man: "A man that hath no virtue in himself, ever envieth virtue in others. For men's minds will either feed upon their own good or upon others' evil; and who wanteth the one will prey upon the other; and whoso is out of hope to attain to another's virtue, will seek to come at even hand by depressing another's fortune."[21] Literary convention describes such a character as a malcontent. And of course, Iago's descent from the Vice of the morality play points to his role as subtle Machiavel. Finally, Iago himself calls attention to his avenging character:

> [N]othing can or shall content my soul
> Till I am even'd with him, wife for wife;
> Or failing so, yet that I put the Moor
> At least into a jealousy so strong
> That judgment cannot cure. (II.i.298–302)

Whatever motivates Iago and however he may be categorized, it seems apparent that his strategy is to "feminize" his position by adopting the slippery and indefinite nature attributed to woman. We see this most obviously in the role he assumes as Othello's comforter and confidante, the functions that a good wife provides for her husband. This facilitating role subsequently serves as the basis for Iago's appropriation of witchcraft practices, which the Renaissance associated almost entirely with women.

That Renaissance England was a patriarchal society, and defined itself as such, is obvious from its discourse. Although domestic handbooks (which were directed primarily to the gentry and upper classes) often presented mutuality as a substantive aspect of the relationship between husband and wife, the subordination of wife to husband was a much stronger concept, primarily, it seems, because the woman's sphere of the home of necessity fashioned her into a private refuge for her husband, whose occupation was invariably public.[22] As long ago as 1919 Alice Clark argued that the social and economic position of women declined throughout the seventeenth century, and social historians have recently suggested that this decline may have begun in the sixteenth century.[23]

Such subordination carries with it certain powers, as is evident in the following passage from Vives's *Instruction of a Christen Woman:*

> The wife should *couple and binde* her husbande unto her everie daye more and more, with her pleasant & gentle conditions, . . . for nothing doth more *draw & entice* unto it, than doth pleasant conditions & sweet speech. A wise woman should have in mind merry tales, & histories (howbeit yet honest) wherewith she may refresh her husband, & make him merry when he is weary. And also shee shall learn precepts of wisdome to exhort him unto virtue, or draw him from vice with all, and some sage sentences against the assaults and rages of both fortunes, both to *plucke downe* her husbands stomacke, if hee be proud of prosperity and wealth: and *comfort and heart* him, if he be stricken in heaviness with adversitie.[24]

What is interesting about this passage is that Vives locates a wife's power in rhetorical skill: through her ability to read her husband's mood and to respond with appropriate verbal decorum (story, advice, admonition, or comfort), a woman *binds* her husband to her self. Normally it is woman's *silence* that is praised, not her powers of persuasion, for of course rhetoric is highly manipulative and can work to empower the wife at the expense of the husband's authority.

This is exactly what happens in act III's temptation scene. Iago, already Othello's military subordinate, takes a lesson from the marriage manuals of the day and gains power over his superior by pretending dutiful compliance and concern. Through brilliant rhetorical positioning and an instinctive sense of his audience's changing responses, he convinces Othello of

Desdemona's unfaithfulness. And he does so, as I have pointed out, by persuading Othello that Desdemona is being deliberately deceitful, that she is in fact a kind of witch. In reality, Iago himself is the witch, apparently dominated by the power structure but insidiously working to subvert it by co-opting the power strategy of woman.

It is logical that Iago would feel comfortable using such a strategy. Fiedler points out that "exploited outsiders"—in this case, a disgruntled sergeant and the entire female sex—"tend to resemble each other strangely."[25] That Iago feels marginalized in the world of the play is obvious from the very first scene. In his discussion with Roderigo, Iago complains that Othello has passed him over for promotion. Even if we believe that Iago is playacting for Roderigo, his bitter resentment at not being offered the job is clear. "I know my price," says Iago, "I am worth no worse a place" (I.i.11). Cassio, "a great arithmetician" who has no battlefield experience, is the choice, and Iago, "his Moorship's ancient." The world works according to the so-called old boy network, says Iago, and I—honest, plain Iago—am not part of that system. Although Iago may have the battlefield experience that Cassio does not, it certainly is not true that he is a simple innocent, unconnected to the movers and shakers of the world, for he says at the beginning of the speech that "three great ones of the city" spoke to Othello personally for him. Consequently, Iago shows himself not unsophisticated about how the world works. What is true, however, is that Iago's conception of himself as a man who can climb easily through the ranks (which is how he has fashioned himself to be) has been violated. Therefore, he determines to get even.

Iago offers many reasons for his dissatisfaction beyond his failure to get the lieutenantship—that Othello has cuckolded him, that Cassio has cuckolded him, that he (Iago) is in love with Desdemona, that Cassio "hath a daily beauty in his life / That makes [himself] ugly" (V.i.19–20). The common factor in all these reasons is that Iago somehow feels powerless, impotent, displaced—an outsider looking in. Othello is an obvious target for Iago's hatred because of his place in the Venetian power structure: he is Iago's superior, the one who has passed Iago over for a promotion; as a Moor, he himself is an alien, but one who has been accepted by the establishment; and finally, Othello "is of a free and open nature, / That thinks men honest that but seem to be so" (I.iii.399–400). Along with these characteristics that distinguish Othello from Iago, however, are also several similarities: both men are soldiers of the field; both are outsiders in Venice, Othello because of race and Iago because of class; and both try to advance themselves, Othello through his military prowess and his marriage to a Venetian woman and Iago through military promotion.[26] Thus Othello, simultaneously unlike and like Iago, becomes the logical focus for the sergeant's bitter dissatisfaction.

His soliloquies in act I, scene iii, and in act II, scenes i and iii, reveal that Iago creates his plot against Othello as circumstances change; his improvisational ability is his power, as Stephen Greenblatt reminds us.[27] This changeability, however, as Iago himself points out to Othello when he is slandering Desdemona in act III, scene iii, differentiates woman from man. Of course, changeability is associated with woman primarily because her nature is cold and wet, and this physiology affects her psychological stability,[28] making her more susceptible to the temptations of the devil, for example. Consequently, in exhibiting this "feminine" trait of changeability, Iago simultaneously dissociates himself from the masculine establishment he undermines and links himself with devilish practices, thus marking himself a witch. Along with this behavioral identification, Iago also verbally links himself with hell and the devil several times during the play (I.iii.357, 403–4; II.iii.350–53), and Othello too makes this connection in act V, scene ii (V.ii.286–87, 301–2). Further, the words that Iago uses to tempt Othello may be likened to the charms that witches were said to use, spells that disrupted order and engendered chaos: in this case, Othello destroys himself by destroying his marriage.[29]

Iago performs several other functions that are linked to devilish practices. First, he prevents Othello and Desdemona from consummating their marriage, interrupting them in Venice, then on their first night in Cyprus,[30] and finally on the second night in Cyprus, when Othello murders Desdemona on their marriage bed. Such interruption of marital consummation is commonly attributed to witches in various manuals. Second, the parodic marriage service in act III, scene iii, actually inverts the Christian ceremony, because Othello the "husband" is being ruled by Iago the "wife," and because the ceremony serves evil and death rather than the Christian virtues of love and life.[31] Likewise, the brothel scene of act IV, scene ii, transmutes the meeting of a husband and wife joined in true marriage into an obscene liaison between a prostitute and her customer. And finally, Iago convinces Othello that his brutal murder of Desdemona will be an act of justice, not the inhuman and monstrous deed that it is (V.ii). Such inversion of ritual is a mark of witchcraft practices, which turn topsy-turvy everything associated with the Christian God and His worship, especially the sacraments, in order to subvert His authority.[32]

The "feminizing" nature of Iago's strategy—his adoption of "wifely" tactics as a mask for his improvising and shape-changing and his co-option of the female crime of witchcraft—problematizes his gender: first, in relation to Othello, and second, in relation to the masculine power structure of the Venetian state. In taking Othello away from Desdemona, in turning him toward a world antagonistic to the moral world he had been inhabiting, Iago is "other," a kind of demon lover—but, I would argue, in metaphor, not in reality. Those scholars who have seen Iago as sexually attracted to his general might use the witchcraft evidence as proof for their own position. However, I interpret the homosexual reading of Iago as an inference resulting from the strategy that Iago uses against Othello, instead of the strategy being a sign of his homosexuality.

If Iago cannot accurately be labeled a homosexual, his role as demon lover nevertheless does not dispel questions about his gender identity: on the one hand, he admits a love/lust for Desdemona, but on the other hand, he "marries" Othello. A more appropriate assessment of the relationship between Iago and Othello is to acknowledge its homosocial qualities, to openly admit Iago's simultaneous attraction to and repulsion from his general, and to recognize his use of Desdemona's body—and her function as wife—as a battleground for his conflicted psyche.[33] This internalized gender warfare glosses the long-noted sexual tensions at play in *Othello:* the sexual politics of husband and wife, apparent in the marriages of both Iago and Emilia and Othello and Desdemona, as well as in Cassio's treatment of Bianca, and also the portrayal of three women characters who threaten the masculine order—one falsely accused of adultery, another a prostitute, and the third a shrew. Affective heterosexual bonding, the conventional norm for sexual coupling, is evident only in the parodic sense, in the "unholy alliance" between Iago and Othello.[34] The other relationships between the sexes exhibit only misogyny, patriarchal tyranny, and tragic alienation.

Iago's "feminine" strategy finally discloses a larger cultural anxiety about gender. For although Iago defines himself in totally masculine categories—beshrewed husband, experienced soldier, loyal comrade-in-arms—his dissatisfaction with his world and his devious machinations against it call into question his gender identification and his allegiance to patriarchal society. This gender confusion within the character of Iago supports a current hypothesis argued by several Renaissance scholars who recently have noted that the public relationship of courtier to prince is often represented in terms of private heterosexual relationships. For example, Frank Whigham and Arthur Marotti have argued that the political and socioeconomic relationship of courtier to monarch is inscribed in the erotic language of the love sonnet.[35] Iago, in practicing such humanist-approved behavior, subverts the power structure such behavior should be reinforcing. The text of *Othello* portrays stereotypically feminine strategies of power as the ultimate weapon against the male prerogative: the patriarchy, self-defined as open and straightforward, cannot defend itself against what it sees as the inherent guile and subtlety of the feminine nature.

In conclusion, the witchcraft paradigm offers more to *Othello* than a neutral description for Iago's subversive behavior: its nature as a female crime complicates Iago's professed masculinity, and thus his relationship to Othello and the patriarchal Venetian state. This gender anxiety is given shape in a parodic love triangle, in which Iago is balanced between Othello and Desdemona, collapsing the roles of adulterer and witch into that of demon lover, while at the same time accusing the woman of doing exactly this. Co-opting what he sees as the power of woman—her apparent powerlessness—Iago infiltrates the established order that dominates him and controls his life and shatters it from within by "feminizing" himself. By doing this, he simultaneously lays bare the fictions of male-female relations and problematizes the private and public relationships between men. Sociopath, malcontent, envious man—however Iago may be categorized, his strategy defines him as a witch.

NOTES

Grateful acknowledgment is made to Cornell University Library. I would also like to thank the Humanities Program and Women's Studies Program of Arizona State University for grant support in the writing of this essay.

1. Although other critics, particularly Robert B. Heilman in his *Magic in the Web: Action and Language in "Othello"* (Lexington: University of Kentucky Press, 1956), have examined how the metaphor of witchcraft operates in the language and action of *Othello,* only David Kaula has examined the function of witchcraft in the play as a specific historical activity. In "Othello Possessed: Notes on Shakespeare's Use of Magic and Witchcraft," *Shakespeare Studies* 2 (1966): 112–32, Kaula identifies the supernatural in *Othello* as the ground from which "love and hate and their attendant feelings . . . arise and into which they ultimately recede" (127). Although I share Kaula's view of Shakespeare's use of witchcraft, I argue here that the gender-specific nature of the crime offers us a window onto Iago's plottings. For a fascinating discussion of how assertive femininity and blackness were linked in the Renaissance mind-set as being "monstrous" (and, therefore, linked to the devil), see Karen Newman, " 'And wash the Ethiop white': Femininity and the Monstrous in *Othello,* " in *Shakespeare Reproduced,* ed. Jean E. Howard and Marion F. O'Connor (New York: Methuen, 1987), 143–62. Rather than emphasizing the actual treatment of witches, I focus on the aesthetic use to which Shakespeare put witchcraft practices in *Othello,* particularly in his construction of character and of power and gender relations.

2. All references to *Othello* are from the *Riverside Shakespeare,* ed. G. Blakemore Evans (Boston: Houghton Mifflin, 1974), unless otherwise noted. I have omitted the brackets in the *Riverside* text, which indicate a reading emended in the copytext.

3. For a discussion of witchcraft practices in England, see two older but still useful studies: Wallace Notestein, *A History of Witchcraft in England* (1911; reprint, New York: Thomas Y. Crowell, 1965); and George Lyman Kittredge, *Witchcraft in Old and New England* (Cambridge: Harvard University Press, 1929). Alan Macfarlane's *Witchcraft in Tudor and Stuart England* (1970; reprint, New York: Harper and Row,

1971) focuses on Essex; Keith Thomas's *Religion and the Decline of Magic* (New York: Scribner's, 1971) addresses all aspects of magic and the occult. Robert H. West's *Reginald Scot and Renaissance Writings on Witchcraft* (Boston: Twayne, 1984) places that very important skeptic's writings in relation to the philosophical and practical treatments of witches. In a background chapter on magic in *The Magician in English Renaissance Drama* (Columbia: University of Missouri Press, 1984), Barbara Howard Traister supplements West's *The Invisible World* (Athens: University of Georgia Press, 1939), which provides a comprehensive survey of the use of magic and the occult in drama.

4. Thomas Cooper, *The Mystery of Witchcraft* (London: Nicholas Okes, 1617), 158; see also 181 (Cornell University Library, Witchcraft BF1581.A2C77).

5. Thomas, *Religion*, 519–26; Joseph Klaits, *Servants of Satan: The Age of the Witch Hunts* (Bloomington: Indiana University Press, 1985), 17–18.

6. Cooper, *Mystery*, 206. Ambition and rebellion are normally recognized as secondary reasons for women's attraction to witchcraft, the foremost being woman's sexual insatiability (which Cooper also asserts). This commonplace was given currency in Heinrich Kramer and James Sprenger's *Malleus maleficarum* (part 1, question 6), first published in 1486 (see the translation by Montague Summers [1928; reprint, London: Arrow Books, 1971], 41–48). Modern historians offer several reasons why women were persecuted as witches more often than were men: their functions as cooks, healers, and midwives; their physical and political weakness; "men's inhumanity to women" (Klaits, *Servants*, 51); "specific aspects of the Reformation period in general and Protestant ideology in particular" (Allison P. Coudert, "The Myth of the Improved Status of Protestant Women: The Case of the Witchcraze," in *The Politics of Gender in Early Modern Europe*, ed. Jean R. Brink, Allison P. Coudert, and Maryanne C. Horowitz [Kirksville, Mo.: Sixteenth Century Journal Publishers, 1989], 63). In *The Witch-Hunt in Early Modern Europe* (London: Longman, 1987), Brian Levack offers a brief bibliography for the relationship of women and witchcraft (243). See also Klaits, *Servants*, especially chapter 3; Carolyn Matalene, "Women as Witches," *International Journal of Women's Studies* 1 (1978): 573–87; and Mary Nelson, "Why Witches Were Women," in *Women: A Feminist Perspective*, ed. Jo Freeman (Palo Alto, Calif.: Mayfield, 1975), 335–68.

7. Thomas, *Religion*, 442.

8. For example, see Alvin Kernan, "Introduction to *Othello*," in *The Complete Signet Classic Shakespeare*, ed. Sylvan Barnet (New York: Harcourt Brace Jovanovich, 1972), 1090–95.

9. Lynda E. Boose, "The Father and the Bride in Shakespeare," *PMLA* 97 (1982): 331–32; Diane Elizabeth Dreher, *Domination and Defiance: Fathers and Daughters in Shakespeare* (Lexington: University Press of Kentucky, 1986), 44–46.

10. In *The Stranger in Shakespeare* (New York: Stein and Day, 1972), Leslie A. Fiedler makes the same point, noting that the genres of comedy and tragedy are formed by the patriarchy's reaction to the daughter's decision to marry: comedy, if the father accepts the daughter's marriage, tragedy if not (145). See also Carol Thomas Neely's review of scholarship on this point: *Broken Nuptials in Shakespeare's Plays* (New Haven: Yale University Press, 1985), 233, n. 16.

11. [Heinrich Bullinger], *The christen state of matrimony* (London: J. Mayler, for J. Gough, 1546), G2v.

12. Michael Neill anticipates my observation in two important articles: see "Changing Places in 'Othello,'" *Shakespeare Survey* 37 (1984): 122; and especially "Unproper Beds: Race, Adultery, and the Hideous in *Othello,*" *Shakespeare Quarterly* 40 (1989): 383–412, for his fascinating linking of adultery and racism.

13. Stephen Greenblatt's argument that Othello's "excessive" love for Desdemona would have constituted adultery according to both Catholic and Protestant religious doctrine offers another perspective for Othello's sexual anxiety. See *Renaissance Self-Fashioning* (Chicago: University of Chicago Press, 1980), 246–49.

14. Marguerite Waller, "Usurpation, Seduction, and the Problematics of the Proper: A 'Deconstructive,' 'Feminist' Rereading of the Seductions of Richard and Anne in Shakespeare's *Richard III,*" in *Rewriting the Renaissance,* ed. Margaret W. Ferguson, Maureen Quilligan, and Nancy J. Vickers (Chicago: University of Chicago Press, 1986), 160.

15. Rodney Poisson, "Death for Adultery: A Note on *Othello,* III.iii.394–96," *Shakespeare Quarterly* 28 (1977): 89–92.

16. George Gifford, *A Discourse of the subtill Practises of Deuilles by VVitches and Sorcerers* (London: T. Orwin, for T. Cooke, 1587), H3r (Cornell University Library, Witchcraft BF1565.G45D5). See also Barbara Rosen, "Introduction," in *Witchcraft,* Stratford-Upon-Avon Library, vol. 6 (London: Edward Arnold, 1969), 18; and Thomas, *Religion,* 531.

17. For a fuller discussion of adultery as a kind of cultural displacement for witchcraft, see Nancy A. Gutierrez, "Philomela Strikes Back: Adultery and Mutilation as Female Self-Assertion," *Women's Studies* 16 (1989): 429–43.

18. Gifford, *Discourse,* H2v.

19. Fred West, "Iago the Psychopath," *South Atlantic Bulletin* 43, no. 2 (1978): 27–35; Martin Wangh, "*Othello:* The Tragedy of Iago," *Psychoanalytic Quarterly* 19 (1950): 202–12; Gordon Ross Smith, "Iago the Paranoiac," *American Imago* 16 (1959): 155–67.

20. Norman N. Holland, *Psychoanalysis and Shakespeare* (1964; reprint, New York: Octagon, 1976), 246–50.

21. Francis Bacon, "Of Envy," in *Selected Writings,* ed. Hugh G. Dick (New York: Modern Library, 1955), 24.

22. Social historians are in the midst of an ongoing dialogue about the nature of the husband-wife relationship in the early modern period. For an argument emphasizing the patriarchal qualities in upper-class marriages, see Lawrence Stone, *The Family, Sex, and Marriage in England, 1500–1800* (New York: Harper and Row, 1977), 151–218. For an argument focusing on the affective ties between husband and wife, see Alan Macfarlane, *Marriage and Love in England, 1300–1840* (Oxford: Basil Blackwell, 1986), especially 174–208. For an analysis of the theories espoused by Catholic and Protestant marriage handbooks, see Kathleen M. Davies, "Continuity and Change in Literary Advice on Marriage," in *Marriage and Society: Studies in the Social History of Marriage,* ed. E. B. Outhwaite (New York: St. Martin's Press, 1981), 58–80. Ralph A. Houlbrooke's *The English Family, 1450–1700* (London: Longman,

1984)—already somewhat dated given the extensive attention this subject has received—offers a good overview of the various methodologies used by family historians, as well as a good summary of conclusions.

23. See Alice Clark, *Working Life of Women in the Seventeenth Century* (1919; reprint, London: Routledge & Kegan Paul, 1982), 1–13, for a summary of her conclusions. See also Joan Kelly-Gadol, "Did Women Have a Renaissance?" in *Becoming Visible,* ed. Renate Bridenthal and Claudia Koonz (Boston: Houghton Mifflin, 1977), 137–64; Stone, *Family,* 195–206; and Merry E. Wiesner, "Women's Defense of Their Public Role," in *Women in the Middle Ages and the Renaissance,* ed. Mary Beth Rose (Syracuse: Syracuse University Press, 1986), 1–27.

24. Quoted in Ruth Kelso, *Doctrine for the Lady of the Renaissance* (Urbana: University of Illinois Press, 1956), 108–9, my emphasis.

25. Fiedler, *Stranger,* 167.

26. Kay Stockholder, *Dream Works: Lovers and Families in Shakespeare's Plays* (Toronto: University of Toronto Press, 1987), 94–99.

27. Greenblatt, *Renaissance,* 222–54.

28. Ian Maclean, *The Renaissance Notion of Woman* (Cambridge: Cambridge University Press, 1980), 28–46, especially 41–44.

29. Kaula, "Othello," 116. See also Edward A. Snow, "Sexual Anxiety and the Male Order of Things in *Othello,*" *English Literary Renaissance* 10 (1980): 384–412, who turns on its head the conventional reading of Othello as being consumed by his bestial nature, arguing instead that Othello, in killing Desdemona, follows the civilizing side of his psyche (superego) not the bestial (id).

30. The text offers no clue as to whether consummation took place on this second night, but when Desdemona asks Emilia to put her wedding sheets on the bed at the end of the play, the implication seems clear that Desdemona and Othello's sexual union had been interrupted. See also T. G. A. Nelson and Charles Haines, "Othello's Unconsummated Marriage," *Essays in Criticism* 33 (1983): 1–18.

31. In "Iago's Satanic Marriage," *McNeese Review* 21 (1974–75): 20–27, Robert F. Willson, Jr., recognizes Iago as a kind of demon lover who makes up a third point on a "love" triangle with Othello and Desdemona, but he does not place this activity within the larger framework of Iago's witchlike machinations.

32. Kaula, "Othello," 119.

33. For a provocative reading of the emblematic significance of the woman's body in the Renaissance as an ideological battleground, see Peter Stallybrass, "Patriarchal Territories: The Body Enclosed," in Ferguson et al., *Rewriting,* 123–42. Closer examination of the male rivalry in *Othello* as homophobia is needed. Eve Kosofsky Sedgwick points out that, in conceptualizations of heterosexual culture and patriarchy, power relations are always exercised between men, whereas women serve as the medium of exchange, as the dominated. In such a world, "a secular, psychologized homophobia ... would be a pivotal and embattled concept ...," particularly in the world of the military, where "the *pre*scription of the most intimate male bonding and the *pro*scription of ... 'homosexuality'" are close to absolute ("The Beast in the Closet: James and the Writing of Homosexual Panic," in *Sex, Politics, and Science in the Nineteenth-Century Novel,* ed. Ruth Bernard Yeazell,

Selected Papers from the English Institute, 1983–84, n.s., 10 [Baltimore: Johns Hopkins University Press, 1986], 150, 152). Sedgwick is referring specifically to the modern military, but her conclusions are also pertinent to the world of *Othello,* which is totally dominated by the military. Given that in the Renaissance homosexuality "was not conceived as part of the created order at all" (Bray, *Homosexuality in Renaissance England,* quoted in Sedgwick, "Beast," 149), Iago's metaphoric displacement of Desdemona as demon lover thus plays out his homophobic panic in relation to Othello. For a full description of Sedgwick's theory, see *Between Men: English Literature and Male Homosocial Desire* (New York: Columbia University Press, 1985).

34. This parody of heterosexual relationships in *Othello* was suggested to me in reading Nancy Vickers, " 'The Blazon of Sweet Beauty's Best': Shakespeare's *Lucrece,* " in *Shakespeare and the Question of Theory,* ed. Patricia Parker and Geoffrey Hartman (New York: Methuen, 1985), 95–115: "Here, metaphors commonly read as signs of a battle between the sexes emerge rather from a homosocial struggle . . . " (96).

35. Frank Whigham, *Ambition and Privilege* (Berkeley: University of California Press, 1984), and "Sexual and Social Mobility in *The Duchess of Malfi,* " *PMLA* 100 (1985): 167–86; Arthur Marotti, " 'Love Is Not Love': Elizabethan Sonnet Sequences and the Social Order," *ELH* 49 (1982): 396–428. See also Kelly-Gadol, "Did Women," and Stallybrass, "Patriarchal."

Thomas Middleton's Antifeminist Sentiment in *A Mad World, My Masters*

FUMIKO TAKASE

"To dote on weakness, slime, corruption, woman!"[1]

It is not surprising that antifeminist sentiment pervades Thomas Middleton's play *A Mad World, My Masters,* for the persistent association of woman with lust and the devil was part of Middleton's cultural heritage. Many classical dramas, those of Euripides and Seneca, for example, were based on antagonism between the sexes. Satire is often directed against women; Aristophanes, Juvenal, and Semonides of Amorgus all attacked women in their works. Christian mythology and iconography also shaped attitudes toward women by helping to develop the polarity between Eve and the Virgin Mary: "Sin came into the world through a woman: redemption became possible because a woman was God's mother on earth.... Eve-baiting became the sport of the moralists, and was not seriously counteracted by the cult of the Virgin Mary, which began in the early centuries and reached its peak in the twelfth."[2] Chaucer's Wife of Bath refutes the medieval views on women, such as the juxtaposition of woman's love with hell, with barren land where water will not dwell, with unruly fire, and with the destruction of her spouse. She declares that God gave women "deceite, wepyng, spynnyng" as weapons.[3]

However, even in the Middle Ages women occasionally had been praised, just as there were Elizabethans who continued to attack them.[4] Alexander Barclay, translating Sebastian Brant, writes of "disordred loue and veneryous": "Suffre not your soules damned and lost to be / By vayne lust and carnall sensualyte."[5] Thomas Nashe exposes to its ugliest reality the association of lust, venereal disease, and sin: "Men and women that haue gone vnder the South pole, must lay off their furde night-caps in spight of their teeth, and become yeomen of the Vineger bottle: a close periwig hides all the sinnes of an olde whore-master; but *Cucullus non facit Monachum:* 'tis not their newe bonnets will keepe them from the old boan-ach. Ware when a mans sins are written on his ey-browes, and that there is not a haire bredth betwixt them and the falling sicknes."[6] John Marston's court bawd, Maquerelle, professes: "Why, that at four women were fools; at fourteen, drabs; / at forty, bawds; at fourscore, witches; and at a hundred, cats."[7] She instructs ladies in the supreme importance of their appearance: "Let men say what they will. Life o' woman! They are ignorant of your wants. The more in years, the more in perfection they grow; if they lose youth and beauty, they gain wisdom and discretion. But when our beauty fades, goodnight with us! There cannot be an uglier thing to see than an old woman, from which—O pruning, pinching, and painting!—deliver all sweet beauties!"[8]

Middleton catches the tone of contemporary diatribes against women in *A Mad World, My Masters,* where he attaches more naturalistic and physiological images to women than to men. Disguising himself as his grandfather's whore, Follywit, the protagonist, regards woman as a kind of hell's mouth representing greed and lechery: "To / drink down a man, she that should set him up, pray is not that / monstrously against kind, now?" (III.iii.93–95). Indeed, he thinks of sexuality in relation to drinking and eating. In love with the Courtesan, Frank Gullman, Follywit wishes that "I might be hang'd if my love do not stretch to her / deeper and deeper" and feels an increase of sexual appetite at her pretended coyness: "When there comes a restraint on't, upon flesh, we / are always most greedy upon't, and that makes your / merchant's wife oftentimes pay so dear for a mouthful" (IV.v.51–52, 53–55).

The connection between sex and biological functioning inevitably implies mortality. Follywit accepts his comrade Mawworm's description of him as "a piece of clay": "Clay! Dost call thy captain clay? Indeed, clay was made to / stop holes, he says true" (III.iii.112, 113–14). The juxtaposition of the idea of mortal man as clay with that of "holes" also links the grave with the genital holes, which again goes back to the speech Follywit's grandsire, Sir Bounteous, makes when he visits the Courtesan and hears that she is sick: "I / was lusty when I came in, but I am down now, i' faith. / Mortality! Yea, this puts me in mind of a hole seven foot / deep, my grave, my grave, my grave" (III.ii.23–26). Another character, the cuckold Harebrain, urges the Courtesan, who pretends to be a virtuous advisor, to have his wife read the chapter on hell in the Jesuit Robert Parsons's *Resolution,* where there is written "the horrible punishments for / itching wantonness, the pains allotted for adultery" (I.ii.50–51). Later, he warns her, " 'Tis only lechery that's damn'd to th' pit-hole" (I.ii.133).

The association of feminine carnality with the devil is nowhere more strongly illustrated than in Penitent Brothel's denunciation of women: man's lust is a "natural drunkard" that "makes our shame apparent in our fall" (IV.i.9, 10), doting on "weakness, slime, corruption, woman" (IV.i.18). Penitent's fall, with "hell and [his] soul . . . mix'd" (IV.i.26), is a metaphor for the Fall of Man, divorced from heaven. He is visited by the Succubus in the shape of the object of his adulterous love, Mistress Harebrain. After this "soul-quaking" (IV.i.71) experience, he wonders, "What knows the lecher when he clips his whore / Whether it be the devil his parts adore?" (IV.iv.55–56) and realizes that the female genitalia are an open door to sin and hell:

> He will keep open still that he commends,
> And there he keeps a table for his friends;
> And she consumes more than his sire could hoard,
> Being more common than his house or board. (IV.iv.66–69)

Although the professional prostitute is a rare character in Shakespeare's plays and even Jonson's (except Dol Common in *The Alchemist*), for Middleton the Courtesan is the embodiment of human corruption. She stands for the aggregation of lust, greed, and vanity, epitomizing the pit of hell into which all the other characters are enticed to fall.

The world of Middleton's play reflects the economic unrest and changing religious and moral values of the Jacobean age.[9] It is as immoral as the worlds of Marston's and Jonson's plays, where grasping overreachers and sharpers scuffle for money, with lust for cash complemented by lust for women. But the latent omnipresence in Middleton's play of the invisible world of damnation and the confused coexistence of carnal and spiritual values indicate that such a mad or unkempt world is ultimately to be judged by traditional religious and moral standards. All the characters are made to bear names representing rigid allegorical character types. Indeed, the work is an extended morality play, with Follywit, Sir Bounteous Progress, the Courtesan, Master and Mistress Harebrain, and Penitent Brothel struggling for vain profits at the peril of their eternal souls. They reveal the fallen state of humankind in the milieu of the so-called city comedies written about 1605–6.

If allegory is of a contrapuntal structure, saying "by this I also mean that,"[10] the action of the play and its characters should be viewed in light of the contrast between what people are and what people should be. In fact, the mad world is a world of enjoyable seeming and antireason, one that totally disregards the disturbing necessities and truths, such as illness and death. Such a world of pleasurable appearances is, in turn, a world of disguise and deceit. The characters disguise themselves so that they may hide their intentions from those whom they want to deceive. The needy Follywit transforms himself into the rich Lord Owemuch, the Courtesan, and a traveling player; the Courtesan, into a chaste and devout virgin; the adulteress Mistress Harebrain, into an obedient and virtuous wife; the adulterer Penitent Brothel, into a doctor and a preacher; and the vain and sexually repulsive Sir Bounteous, into a generous and hospitable Sir Bounteous.

As long as the world of appearances and deceptions lasts, the Courtesan is its presiding genius. Compared by her mother to a spider weaving "her cauls" with art and cunning to entrap flies (I.i.141), Frank Gullman, as her name plainly illustrates, gulls all the other characters. The main plot of lust for ready money, involving Follywit and Sir Bounteous, and the subplot of sexual lust, involving Master and Mistress Harebrain and Penitent Brothel, are combined in the character of the Courtesan, who marries Follywit in the end. She thinks of herself as a park, with Sir Bounteous Progress as its keeper, and boastingly justifies her prostitution: "in / common reason one keeper cannot be enough for so proud a / park as a woman" (I.i.135–37). Her bawd mother testifies that although she has sold her daughter's maidenhead fifteen times, there is still enough maidenhead for old Sir Bounteous. She instructs her daughter in the art of seduction and the importance of appearances: "Who gets th' opinion for a virtuous name / May sin at pleasure, and ne'er think of shame" (I.i.168–69). Her appearance of chastity is produced by reading the Scripture and avoiding "all profane talk, wanton compliments, undecent / phrases, and lascivious courtings" (I.i.183–84). However, it completely entraps customers, such as the elderly brothers, Inesse and Possibility.

The Courtesan's wit can meet any crisis with breathtaking audacity. She cooperates with Penitent by feigning illness so that Mistress Harebrain can get permission from her jealous husband to visit her and thus consummate her own affair with Penitent Brothel. Sir Bounteous and the elderly brothers come before their appointed rendezvous time, but the Courtesan chases them away, one after another. Penitent, disguised as the Courtesan's doctor, admires her art of gulling men: "The wit of man wanes and decreases soon, / But women's wit is ever at full moon" (III.ii.159–60). She pretends to hold a conversation with her visitor from her sickbed while Penitent and Mistress Harebrain are copulating in the next room. Master Harebrain, as giddy and reckless a fool as his name indicates, overhears the seemingly virtuous conversation between his wife, mostly silent, and the Courtesan, her sick friend and advisor, whom he believes to be a maid of the purest virtue. The feigned conversation is full of sexual puns and is well timed to hide the progress of the lovers' activities, while the cuckolded husband listens outside, to his great comfort, without any notion of what is actually going on inside. The simultaneity of the three actions provides a jarring irony with which to gauge how morally perverse these characters are. The Courtesan encourages Mistress Harebrain to fulfill her sexual desire: "You live a lady's life with him, go where you will, ride / when you will, and do what you will" (III.ii.188–89). As the offstage love-making becomes violent, the Courtesan has to account for the noise: "Still, still weeping?—[Sobs.] Huff, huff, huff. —Why, how / now, woman? Hey, hy, hy, for shame, leave. —Suh, suh. / —She cannot answer me for sobbing" (III.ii.197–99). She even verbally feigns fits of ague, and Master Harebrain, out of sight, sympathizes with her: "Poor soul, how she's tormented" (III.ii.206). When his wife and the "doctor" (Penitent) appear, he laughs with satisfaction, believing that he has completely gulled her:

> i'faith, to my great comfort;
> I deceiv'd you there, wife, ha, ha!
> I do entreat thee, nay, conjure thee, wife,
> Upon my love or what can more be said,
> Oft'ner to visit this sick, virtuous maid. (III.ii.237–41)

The Courtesan's attitude toward Follywit's courtship is full of deceit and sexual innuendo, which the young man takes at face value. Her mother testifies to her modesty:

> She could not endure the sight of a man, forsooth,
> But run and hole herself presently. So choice of her
> Honor, I am persuaded whene'er she has husband
> She will e'en be a precedent for all married wives,
> How to direct their actions and their lives. (IV.v.43–47)

She pretends to be what she is not, "a poor and silly virgin," while her mother assures her, "Men love as purely as you can be chaste"; at Follywit's mention of Sir Bounteous, the mother says, "I know your grandsire well; she knows him better" (IV.v.67, 85, 96). Thus, the young man is entrapped in her "cauls" by her appearance of simple modesty "without sophistication" (IV.v.56–57), which he hopes his love to have. Short of cash, Follywit suggests that they go to Sir Bounteous's feast and make it "serve fitly / for [their] wedding dinner" (IV.v.127–28). When at the feast her real nature is exposed with derision by Bounteous and Mawworm, she audaciously demands forgiveness in return for her future obedience: "What I have been is past; be that forgiven, / And have a soul true both to thee and heaven" (V.ii.259–60). When we remember the artful dissembling she has taught to Mistress Harebrain and her mother's assurance that she will be the precedent for all wives, none of us can believe in the Courtesan's instant conversion.

Penitent Brothel, the Courtesan's associate in corrupting the silly housewife, is the only character who is caught in the dilemma between a knowledge of evil and an inability to escape it. Indeed, his role is crucial in understanding Middleton's idea of how humankind, fallen and helpless even though created in the image of God, distorts and bestializes life through uncontrollable sexual impulses. The life of the brothel and the life of religious penitence coexist in Penitent Brothel's name, and he is, in fact, in a dichotomous and "schizoid state."[11] Although Follywit, Sir Bounteous, Frank Gullman, her mother, and the Harebrains belong to the world of appearances, they do not suffer much from their perversion of the traditional moral and religious codes into acts of prostitution, thievery, familial betrayal, cuckoldry, and the violation of holy matrimony. However, at the very beginning of the play, Penitent is already fully conscious that his adulterous love for another man's wife is a damnable sin. Though Penitent describes Follywit's tricks and robberies as "his youth of common receiv'd riot, / Time's comic flashes, and the fruits of blood" (I.i.92–93), he is ashamed of and alarmed at his own carnal appetite, which, even though he knows it will damn him, he still "willingly" embraces (I.i.96).

David Farley-Hills tries to explain this "willingly" in terms of the Calvinistic doctrine of the corrupt will and denies C. A. Hallett's argument that it is after reading Parsons's *Resolution* that Penitent realizes he is "divorc'd from heaven" (IV.i.3).[12] In fact, it is with full knowledge of his future damnation that he plots to meet Mistress Harebrain. His contrivance is to use the Courtesan as the means, "One poison for another," to corrupt and loosen Mistress Harebrain's "most constant powers" (I.i.102, 105), taking advantage of Master Harebrain's trust in the Courtesan disguised as a virtuous advisor. It is, indeed, the most heinous treason against himself and the Harebrains. Middleton presents Penitent's "willing" fall into hell through a multiplicity of foci in the love scene with Mistress Harebrain. Afterwards, his soul, divorced from heaven, draws forth from hell the Succubus in the form of Mistress Harebrain. Against her temptation and her "damn'd art" (IV.i.72), he calls on "Celestial soldiers" and "ministers of faith and grace" to guard him (IV.i. 31, 33). When the devil leaves him, he thinks that he has regained honesty and that there is no need to fear his mistress's husband. He urges the dismayed Mistress Harebrain to virtue: "Be honest; then the devil will ne'er assume thee" (IV.iv.44), and preaches chastity:

> Live honest, and live happy, keep thy vows;
> She's part a virgin whom but one man knows.
> Embrace thy husband, and beside him none;
> Having but one heart, give it but to one. (IV.iv.70–73)

With tears in her eyes and on her knees, Mistress Harebrain swears that no man shall ever wrong her husband's bed, whereupon he comes forward from his hiding place in gratitude: "Two dear rare gems this hour presents me with, / A wife that's modest, and a friend that's right. / Idle suspect and fear, now take your flight" (IV.iv.79–81).

By means of viewpoint and irony (Harebrain's religious sermon on chastity with its sexual implications underneath), Middleton provides the audience with some serious doubt as to the sincerity of Penitent's repentance: is it just a trick to silence his love about their illicit liaison, making a fool of her credulous husband? In the last scene, where it is proved that the real constable, a representative of justice, has been bound by the player-thief

Follywit, Penitent speaks of the comic truth of their topsy-turvy life of deceit and corruption: "We should betray and laugh at our own folly then, for of / my troth none here but was deceiv'd in't" (V.ii.161–62).

In *A Mad World, My Masters* the women are successful in achieving what they want. Mistress Harebrain's adultery is completely forgotten without any visible signs of repentance. The Courtesan becomes Mistress Follywit. Indeed, in the world of appearances "no woman kept so privately but may / watch advantage to make the best of her pleasure" (I.i.134–135), which the Courtesan does, and with unbelievable success. Mistress Harebrain's perverted sexuality is symbolized by the Succubus, and the Courtesan's lust is appropriately linked to Follywit's lust for ready cash.

Follywit, as his name indicates, has the folly to pride himself on his wit (inventiveness), which directs his progress of moral depravity to its terminus, namely, marriage with the Courtesan. In the opening scene he boasts of his "transformation" from the virtuous boy who "went all in black, swore but o' Sundays" (I.i.14) to his present state: "I go without order, swear without / number, gull without mercy, and drink without measure" (I.i.21–22). The only heir to his grandsire Sir Bounteous, a knight of thousands, Follywit decides to cheat him of some of his fortune while he is still alive. He thinks that it is "but a borrowing of so much beforehand" (II.ii.36). His three robberies succeed in spite of his skin-deep disguises. In his first attempt he makes three charges against his grandfather to justify his own robbery and breaking of the family tie—cheating, usury, and extortion: "If ever he did cozen the simple, why I was born to revenge their quarrel; if ever oppress the widow, I, a fatherless child, have done as much for him. And so 'tis through the world either in jest or earnest. Let the usurer look for't; for craft recoils in the end, like an overcharg'd musket, and maims the very hand that puts fire to't. There needs no more but a usurer's own blow to strike him from hence to hell; 'twill set him forward with a vengeance" (III.iii.6–14).

Follywit's trick succeeds as he has hoped, with the better of his alternatives: "I'll either go like a lord as I came, or be hang'd like a thief / as I am" (II.iv.90–91), simply because Sir Bounteous does not want his reputation of hospitality to be spoiled by the rumor that Lord Owemuch has been robbed at his house. However, remembering that his grandfather keeps a quean, he tricks the old man a second time. With the lower part of a gentlewoman's gown, a mask, and a chin-clout, Follywit disguises himself as Sir Bounteous's whore and steals the jewels from his room, then puts the blame on her. Follywit thinks that it is against nature for Sir Bounteous to keep a whore in his "crinkling days" to hinder the young man's intentions. He justifies his unnatural intrigue a second time: "Who keeps a harlot, tell him this from me, / He needs nor thief, disease, nor enemy" (IV.iii.49–50).

He succeeds again simply because of Sir Bounteous's inability to tell his grandson from his quean, though he absurdly recognizes some changes in her, compounded "of wine, beer, and tobacco" (IV.iii.56). The old man denounces the strumpet's love in terms of "a waft i'th' end" (IV.iii.94). In the final scene of the play the fiction of the comedy, ironically entitled *The Slip,* is staged by Follywit to entertain and deceive his grandfather, but the action of the play within the play is so confused with the world of the framing play that the real constable, who comes in to arrest Follywit as a thief whom he has caught riding off with Sir Bounteous's properties—"a chain, a jewel, and a watch" (V.ii.215)—is bound and gagged as part of *The Slip.* Follywit is about to get the third success in his invention and jest when the watch rings alarum in his pocket. Proven guilty of the robbery, he suffers the worse humiliation of discovering himself married to his grandfather's whore. Follywit, "a mad-brain o'th' first, whose pranks scorn to have / precedents," and "whose only glory is to be prime of the company" (I.i.83–84, 87), is now showered with derision, not only from his grandfather, but also from his wild "consorts," who must have known his new wife better than their "captain" knew her. Here, Penitent's comment, "He's the carrion, and they the kites that gorge upon him" (I.i.89), comes alive for him.

Sir Bounteous tolerates having his whore, who has betrayed him, and her bawd mother at his feast. As his name reveals, he is a man of bounteous disposition, whose "humor" is to feast his neighbors, welcome Lord Owemuch to stay at his house, and compensate him for his loss due to burglary. He boasts to Owemuch (Follywit in disguise) of his generosity to his grandson—his love, his tolerance for his "pranks," and his intended conveyance to him of his fortune—but at the same time he does not hide his contempt for him: "*Imberbis juvenis,* his chin has no more prickles / yet than a midwife's" (II.i.126–27). As long as he lives, "the whoreson" shall never have his money. Though David Farley-Hills says that "in many ways Sir Bounteous acts like the festal king, converting discord into harmony and dispute into reconciliation,"[13] Sir Bounteous's speech and behavior are not entirely void of pride, vanity, and malice. As Una Ellis-Fermor argues, his "charity begins abroad and ends at home";[14] he vainly prides himself on his hospitality as an art that no knight in the shire can exceed: "I warrant ye there's not one knight i'th' shire able to entertain a lord i'th' cue, or a lady i'th' nick like me, like me. There's a kind of grace belongs to't, a kind of art which naturally slips from me, I know not on't, I promise you, 'tis gone before I'm aware on't." (II.i.53–58) Standish Henning notes Sir Bounteous's "egocentrism that lurks behind his delight in hospitality."[15] The pronoun "I" and its variants haunt this mock humility: with them he can circle back to himself as frequently as he wishes. Because of his egocentrism, Sir Bounteous pays off the losses that Lord Owemuch has suffered in order not to have his reputation for hospitality damaged and decides that the stealing committed by "the courtesan" (Follywit again in disguise) "must slip and sleep . . . / Because [his] credit shall not lose her luster" (IV.iii.100, 102).

Ready to be horrified occasionally by disturbing truths of life, such as plagues and death, Sir Bounteous always looks outward to things that please his appetites, both palatal and sexual. Boasting to Lord Owemuch of his rich Venetian curtains, which describe the biblical story of the prodigal son, he tells him that the swine are left out of the scene "for spoiling the curtains" (II.ii.7). However, there is an unpleasant moment of epiphany when, while visiting the brothel where his courtesan resides and hearing the report of her sickness, he fears that she might have been stricken with the plague. The image of "a hole seven foot / deep" frightens him out of his lusty dream, but when the doctor/Penitent denies that the Courtesan has any such disease, Sir Bounteous instantly congratulates himself, despite his sexual incompetency, for having got her with child. His vain egocentrism is well described by Frank Gullman: "How soon he took occasion / to slip into his own flattery, soothing his own defects" (III.ii.85–86). When he thinks that his whore has proved "a thieving quean" (IV.iii.85), he momentarily recognizes his fault in spending money on her while starving his heir apparent:

> Did she want anything? Was she not supplied?
> Nay, and liberally, for that's an old man's sin;
> We'll feast our lechery though we starve our kin.
> Is not my name Sir Bounteous? Am I not express'd there?
> Ah, fie, fie, fie, fie, fie. (IV.iii.88–92)

Sir Bounteous denounces the Courtesan in terms of "a waft" on his tongue. As an act of repayment for Follywit's tricks and marriage with his whore, he generously offers Follywit a gift of money, appropriately described in terms of palatal taste, vainly proud that he is the one who has sipped the top and left the unsavory bottom for his heir apparent: "And since I drink the top, take her; and hark, / I spice the bottom with a thousand mark" (V.ii.263–64). Both grandfather and son are, indeed, of the same blood, thinking of woman in terms of the physiological function of drinking, which every living creature has to do to live. Follywit, who had scorned love as the "high height of madness full" (IV.v.13) and believed that only "a woman's simple modesty" (IV.v.64) would move his heart, is now aware that he has been gulled by the Courtesan's appearance just as Sir Bounteous has been gulled by his nephew's disguises. Because it is futile to deny the truth at this point, the young man proves himself a worthy heir to the old man's vanity, lechery, and taste, and accepts his gifts—his whore and money—jovially:

> By my troth, she is as good a cup of nectar as any bachelor needs to sip at.
> Tut, give me gold, it makes amends for vice;
> Maids without coin are caudles without spice. (V.ii.265–68)

In the end, Follywit evaluates women in terms of drinking, a daily physiological necessity, and what matters to him most is money. It should be remembered that when he marries, he is glad to get her flesh, beauty, and "a dowry of three hundred pound" (IV.v.112), with which he might survive until Sir Bounteous's death. He puts his lust for ready money above love, both filial and amatory, which brings him down to the level of the Courtesan in the same way that Penitent's lust for Mistress Harebrain drags him down to the level of the Succubus. Whereas Penitent rejects the devil-woman, Follywit agrees to share his family name with the Courtesan despite the derision and infamy that will be inflicted on him.

Mistress Harebrain is the only character who does not suffer humiliation when her inner perverted sexuality is exposed. Clearly, her fall is of her own making, for the Courtesan assures Penitent: "she's wax of your own / fashioning. She had wrought herself into the form of your / love before my art set finger to her" (I.i.115–17). The chaste-looking housewife is eager "to enjoy his sight" (I.ii.70). Even after Penitent reports the appearance of the Succubus in her form and voice, she does not repent, keeping her reputation for chastity intact.

Through the ironic juxtaposition of viewpoints, the audience knows more about the characters on the stage than the characters do about themselves and about one another; they gaily remain on the pleasing surfaces of their world. Just as Follywit believes that money makes amends for vice, so Sir Bounteous believes that good eating reconciles disputes and strifes. As the festal king who is ready to convert disharmony into harmony, the old man invites all to the feast, recognizing the self-retributive principle in such a world of appearance and deceit:

> Come, gentlemen, to th' feast, let not time waste;
> We have pleas'd our ear, now let us please our taste.
> Who lives by cunning, mark it, his fate's cast;
> When he has gull'd all, then is himself the last. (V.ii.269–72)

Comedy usually ends with the coming of a better world, but here the play ends with the light-hearted recognition of the world as a ship of fools, all possessed by lust. Though T. S. Eliot says that "Middleton has no point of message"[16] and Una Ellis-Fermor says that "he appears to have no rigid moral theory,"[17] the dramatist appeals to the audience's discernment. Middleton's drama is different from Jonson's satire, where the author's voice of judgment is heard everywhere. In Middleton, the silent judgment is the ironic presentation of several viewpoints simultaneously—"by all that is left unsaid."[18]

Names such as Follywit, Sir Bounteous, Penitent, Frank Gullman, and the Harebrains connect Middleton's characters with the tradition of morality plays, where "the devil originated all disguise when he took on himself the form of the snake," and which concluded with "a general stripping of disguise from all the Vices."[19] Although Renaissance comedies patterned after morality plays are often concerned with the sin of lust,[20] Middleton seems to portray only knavery; but a recurring motive for tricks and betrayals is, indeed, lust. By reducing the actions of everyone, men and women, to the single instinct of lust (in Middleton, it should be noted, lust for women and lust for money are one and the same), the dramatist strips humankind of all disguise and portrays the human race as devoid of any passion except lust. As theft and robbery are vices, so is the sexual impulse a manifestation of the devil. Middleton's women are sexually aggressive; they challenge men; they drink down men while their opponents sip and get drunk with women. If women are the pit of hell, men "willingly" fall into it or find money in it. Penitent is the only satiric commentator on the other characters, a position he holds through his awareness of the absurd gap between appearance and reality, between what humanity is and what humanity ought to be, but even he cannot escape from the damnable sin of adultery. There is, indeed, a "coarse and vigorous deromantization of love"[21] and a pathetic parody of holy matrimony in Middleton's play.

The wicked, disguised characters become attractive through their wickedness and inventiveness, whereas sexual relationships and perversions are held as "a subject for laughter rather than a stimulant for the libido."[22] When critics perceive antifeminist sentiment in the play, it is because of the dramatist's "supreme gift, his discernment of the minds of women,"[23] with which he has created such formidable women as the Courtesan, her bawd mother, and Mistress Harebrain, worthy to challenge men in wit, vanity, egoism, and sexuality. All the characters wallow equally in lust, the pit of hell on earth. Just as the morality play ends with the stripping of disguise from Vice, so the finale of *A Mad World, My Masters* ends by stripping all the characters of their disguise, deceit, and pretentiousness. It exposes and condemns them in their ugly, shameless, and sinful reality, to the gay enjoyment of Follywit, Sir Bounteous, Frank Gullman, and others in their separate ways. The world of the play is, in fact, a mad world, as its title indicates. It operates as a tragic "metaphor for the jungle morality,"[24] where traditional religious, social, and moral values are outrageously turned upside down and distorted by lust. However, as Vice in the morality play is finally discomfitted as an object of ridicule, the "world" in *A Mad World, My Masters* is presented as wicked and comic to the audience, whom the dramatist directly addresses as "My Masters" for their intelligent assessment of such a way of life. The spectators, who *"do generally discover everybody's Face but their Own"*[25] in the play, are finally shocked into an awareness that they are involved in the general madness, because, like the play's characters, they eat and drink and express their sexuality. Indeed, the title of the play itself gives Middleton's oblique criticism of the Jacobean world. He creates a world where everyone, he hopes, will discover his or her own face in the play that follows. After all, as man is Adam's son, so woman is Eve's daughter. Both are destined not to rise but to fall, if left to their own bodily concerns.

NOTES

1. Thomas Middleton, *A Mad World, My Masters,* ed. Standish Henning (Lincoln: University of Nebraska Press, 1965), 63 (IV.i.18). All quotations from the play follow this edition.

2. Matthew Hodgart, *Satire* (New York: McGraw-Hill, 1969), 87.

3. Geoffrey Chaucer, "The Canterbury Tales," in *The Works of Geoffrey Chaucer,* ed. F. N. Robinson (London: Oxford University Press, 1974), 80.

4. John Peter, *Complaint and Satire in Early English Literature* (Oxford: Clarendon, 1956), 114.

5. Sebastian Brant, *The Ship of Fools,* 2 vols., trans. Alexander Barclay (New York: AMS [1509] 1966), 1:83.

6. Thomas Nashe, "Pierce Penniless: His Supplication to the Devil," in *The Works of Thomas Nashe,* 5 vols., ed. Ronald B. McKerrow (Oxford: Basil Blackwell, 1958), 1:182.

7. John Marston, *The Malcontent,* ed. M. L. Wine (Lincoln: University of Nebraska Press, 1964), 32 (I.vi.33–35).

8. Marston, *Malcontent,* 50 (II.iv.43–50).

9. L. C. Knights, *Drama and Society in the Age of Jonson* (New York: Barnes & Noble, 1968), 96–269. Knights doubts whether Middleton's comedies are accurate pictures of Jacobean London because of the sameness of the characters from play to play: "The background that he implicitly asks his audience to accept is a world of thriving citizens, needy gallants and landed gentlemen, and fortune-hunters of all kinds—a world that had sufficient basis in actuality to provide some theatrical verisimilitude for his thoroughly improbable plots."

10. Northrop Frye, *Anatomy of Criticism: Four Essays* (Princeton: Princeton University Press, 1971), 90.

11. David Farley-Hills, *The Comic in Renaissance Comedy* (London: Macmillan, 1981), 102.

12. Farley-Hills, *Comic,* 103; cf. C. A. Hallett, "Penitent Brothel, the Succubus and Parsons' *Resolution:* A Reappraisal of Penitent's Position in Middleton's Canon," *Studies in Phililogy* 69 (1972): 79.

13. Farley-Hills, *Comic,* 90.

14. Una Ellis-Fermor, *The Jacobean Drama: An Interpretation* (London: Methuen, 1973), 134.

15. Standish Henning, "Introduction," in Middleton, *A Mad World,* xiv.

16. T. S. Eliot, *Selected Essays* (London: Faber and Faber, 1966), 162.

17. Ellis-Fermor, *Jacobean,* 129.

18. M. C. Bradbrook, *The Growth and Structure of Elizabethan Comedy* (Cambridge: Cambridge University Press, 1979), 157.

19. Ibid., 160.

20. Sylvia D. Feldman, *The Morality-patterned Comedy of the Renaissance* (The Hague: Mouton, 1970), 98.

21. John F. McElroy, *Parody and Burlesque in the Tragicomedies of Thomas Middleton* (Salzburg: Institut für Englische Sprache und Literatur, Universität Salzburg, 1972), 152.

22. Ibid., 22.

23. Ellis-Fermor, *Jacobean,* 149.

24. McElroy, *Parody,* 71.

25. Jonathan Swift, preface to *A Full and True Account of the Battel Fought Last Friday,* in *A Tale of a Tub with Other Early Works, 1696–1707,* ed. Herbert Davis (Oxford: Blackwell, 1965), 140. Here is Swift's famous comparison of satire to *"a sort of Glass, wherein Beholders do generally discover every body's Face but their Own; which is the chief Reason for that kind of Reception it meets in the World, and that so very few are offended with it."*

PART TWO

Refashioning Gender: Appropriating the Amazon

The Only Good Amazon
Is a Converted Amazon: The Woman
Warrior and Christianity in
the *Amadís Cycle*

ALISON TAUFER

Sixteenth-century Spain saw an explosion in Amazon lore, both at home and abroad. As explorers returned from the New World with tales of Amazon tribes, authors such as Garci Rodríguez de Montalvo, Feliciano de Silva, and Pedro de Luján, continuators of the *Amadís Cycle*, were creating a literary tradition of Amazons in the Spanish books of chivalry. Although a renewed interest in Amazons certainly was not unique to Spain during the early modern period, the Amazon appears to have served a special function in Spanish culture at this time. This growth of interest in Amazons parallels the discovery of new peoples in the Western Hemisphere, and it is very possible that the reports of Amazon tribes in Spanish explorers' travel accounts demonstrate a European effort to conceptualize the New World and its inhabitants by contrasting "barbarian" Indian behavior to the Spaniards' own "civilized" behavior. In turn, the portrayal of Amazons in the Spanish books of chivalry mirrors the controversy that surrounded the Indians' status as potential Christians during this period.

This association of Amazons with barbarian peoples has a precursor in ancient Greek tradition, in which Amazons, and the barbarians they represented, are portrayed as meriting conquest and destruction because they threatened Greek values and refused to conform to Greek standards of civilization. However, the Amazons of the sixteenth-century books of chivalry are not destroyed; instead, they convert to Christianity and are welcomed into the Christian community. This concern with conversion instead of destruction reproduces the controversy concerning the New World that raged in Spain at that time over the spiritual status of the Indians. I would like to explore briefly how the Amazon functioned as a metaphor first for the barbarian in ancient Greece and then for the Indian in sixteenth-century Spain. I will then analyze the conversion motif that appears in the

35

Amadís Cycle and explain how it reflects the controversy over the Christianization of the New World Indians.

In ancient Greece, the Amazon became a metaphor for the barbarian in the histories and geographies of such writers as Herodotus, Diodorus Siculus, and Strabo. In these texts, the Amazon serves to explain the forms of social organization practiced by the Greeks' barbarian neighbors. The barbarians' social organization is usually presented as the antithesis of civilized Greek society. Herodotus, for example, credits the social organization of the Sauromatae, a Scythian tribe, to Amazonian ancestors: "Ever since then the women of the Sauromatae have followed their ancient usage; they ride a-hunting with their men or without them; they go to war, and wear the same dress as the men. . . . In regard to marriage, it is the custom that no virgin weds till she has slain a man of the enemy; and some of them grow old and die unmarried, because they cannot fulfil the law."[1] Amazon customs as portrayed in other works, such as Diodorus Siculus and Strabo's *Geography*—male infanticide, female sexual promiscuity, women as warriors and conquerors—invert the values of Greek patriarchal culture. Amazons also represent the threat of barbarian invasion and the potential destruction of Greek civilization. In his *Geography,* Strabo writes: "Who could believe that an army of women, or a city, or a tribe, could ever be organized without men, and not only be organized but even make inroads upon the territory of other people, and not only overpower the peoples near them to the extent of advancing as far as what is now Ionia, but even send an expedition across the sea as far as Attica?"[2]

The response to the Amazonian threat given in the Greek texts is the conquest, domination, and annihilation of the Amazons at the hands of a Greek hero. As Diodorus Siculus puts it: "The race of the Amazons was entirely destroyed by Heracles, when he visited the regions to the west and set up his pillars in Libya, since he felt that it would ill accord with his resolve to be the benefactor of the whole race of mankind if he should suffer any nations to be under the rule of women."[3] To the ancient Greeks, the only good Amazon was a dead Amazon.

In the Renaissance, the Amazon again became a metaphor for the barbarian. The Spanish explorers used the Amazon image to understand and give meaning to their experiences during their explorations. The legends helped them to comprehend, although incorrectly, the customs and forms of social organization that they encountered. As it did for the Greeks, the Amazon figure provided the Spaniards with a model for understanding and dealing with alien cultures by portraying these cultures as the inversion of European civilization. The repeated stories of Amazon sightings in the New World reflected the Europeans' own concerns with Indian cultures: their alternative social orderings, alternative sexual practices, and, of course, their possession of gold.

Columbus, Cortés, Orellana, and others returned from the Americas with stories of Amazons that are almost exact replicas of the earlier Greek accounts of Amazons. Columbus reported the existence of Amazon-like women on the island of Martinio, "which is the first island met on the way from Spain to the Indies, in which there is not a man. These women engage in no feminine occupation, but use bows and arrows of cane."[4] Columbus also mentioned that these women had large amounts of "tuob," which is gold or copper.

Cortés, in his "Fourth Letter" to the emperor, described an island near Ceguatán, "inhabited only by women without any men, and . . . at given times men from the mainland visit them; if they conceive, they keep the female children to which they have given birth, but the males they throw away. This island is ten days' journey from the province. . . . They tell me also that it is very rich in pearls and gold."[5] The priest Juan Díaz, who accompanied Juan de Grijalva in his exploration of the Yucatán coast in 1518, left a report of the expedition that included a reference to Amazons.[6] While exploring the area of Michoacán, Nuño de Guzmán, in a letter dated July 8, 1530, reported the existence of wealthy Amazons who dwelt on an island in the sea and were believed to be goddesses by the local population.[7] Fray Gaspar de Carvajal, a Dominican monk who was part of Francisco de Orellana's 1542 exploration party in the Amazon basin, claimed to have seen Amazons fighting in the area. These women lived without men in the traditional Amazon fashion and possessed vast amounts of gold and silver.[8] The accounts of the Spanish explorers are repetitively similar in that they relate the existence of warlike women who lived without men, disposed of male infants, and possessed large quantities of silver, gold, and precious stones.

As accounts of Amazon communities arrived from the New World, Montalvo, Silva, and Luján were filling their texts with stories of barbarian Amazon queens who fought the Christian forces of Amadís and his ever-increasing progeny. Like the Amazons of the travel accounts, these were warlike women who lived without men, disposed of male infants, and possessed large quantities of silver, gold, and precious stones. However, instead of being destroyed for daring to oppose the powers of goodness and civilization—the fate of their ancestors in the ancient Greek accounts and, indeed, of many New World "barbarians" who had the misfortune to meet with Spanish explorers—the Amazons of these sixteenth-century books of chivalry were joyfully welcomed into the bosom of Mother Church. The sympathetic treatment given Amazons in these books may become more understandable in light of a controversy over the conversion of the Indians that was taking place in Spain during the same historical period.

This controversy, which culminated in the great debate at Valladolid in 1550 between Bartolomé de Las Casas, the Dominican bishop of Chiapas, and the scholar and philosopher Juan Ginés de Sepúlveda, centered on the exact nature of the New World Indians—the barbarians of the sixteenth-century—and whether they were capable of Christianity and European civilization. This controversy may shed some light on the treatment Montalvo, Silva, and Luján each give Amazons in their books of chivalry. These authors continued the tradition of the Amazon myth by portraying Amazons as antithetical to Spanish cultural ideals, but they broke with tradition by converting their Amazons to Christianity rather than destroying them. Although we cannot prove that either Montalvo or Luján knew of the controversy over the status of the Indians, certain facts of Feliciano de Silva's life suggest that Silva may have been aware of this debate. His brother went to the Indies; his son, Diego de Silva, lived in Peru and was godfather to the Inca Garcilaso de la Vega.[9]

The Amazons' behavior in the *Amadís Cycle* includes many of the vices for which Spanish explorers criticized the Indians. For example, in *Sergas de Esplandián,* the Amazons of California are promiscuous and bloodthirsty; they live in caves, practice infanticide, and, ignoring the laws of hospitality, capture and kill unwary travelers.[10] In the *Amadís Cycle,* Amazons are always non-Christians, although they are never Saracens. Their paganism is polytheistic, ranging from the worship of a number of unspecified gods that are referred to simply as *mis dioses* to a belief in the Greco-Roman pantheon. Zahara, who appears in books nine and ten of the cycle (*Amadís de Grecia* and *Florisel de Niquea*), prays to Phoebus, Mars, Venus, and Jupiter and believes herself to have been impregnated by the god Mars.[11]

In *Sergas de Esplandián,* Calafia's Amazon subjects mate promiscuously in the manner of the ancient Amazons. It is important to remember that this practice of random mating is one that is constantly and pointedly attributed to the New World Amazons and most likely reflects the Spaniards' inability to come to terms not only with New World sexual practices but also with the existence of matrilineal family structures.[12]

The most sensational and horrifying vices in the eyes of the Europeans were cannibalism and human sacrifice. The earliest travel accounts, such as those of Columbus and Amerigo Vespucci, portray cannibalism as an everyday occurrence in the Indian way of life. Indians reportedly not only ate their enemies but their own families as well.[13] Although the *Amadís Cycle* contains no man-eating Amazons, the California Amazons of *Sergas de Esplandián* dispose of their male infants by feeding them to pet griffins. They also feed to these animals those men whom they capture on raiding expeditions and those who have had the misfortune to stumble across the Amazons' island. Except that the Amazons themselves do not eat the men,

Montalvo's account of the Amazons' practice of feeding the griffins their male children and their foreign enemies is markedly similar to the accounts of cannibalism reported in sixteenth-century travel literature. The Amazons' treatment of males certainly mirrors the fears of the sixteenth-century Spanish explorers as they pushed even farther into unknown territory.

What was the proper response of a "civilized" nation to such newly found barbaric behavior? Official policy protected the Indians, although this policy remained controversial. Spanish detractors of the Indians advocated slavery or complete destruction; however, they couched their attacks in religious terms. Oviedo, in *Historia general y natural de las Indias,* argues that God had condemned the Indians for their sins and that it was God's will that they be wiped from the face of the earth: "God is going to destroy them soon. . . . Satan has now been expelled from the island [Hispaniola]: his influence has disappeared now that most of the Indians are dead. . . . Who can deny that the use of gunpowder against pagans is the burning of incense to Our Lord."[14] Many detractors believed that the Indians were incapable of Christianity. In 1517, Cardinal Franciso Jiménez de Cisneros stated that "Indians are malicious people who are able to think up ways to harm Christians, but they are not capable of natural judgement or of receiving the faith, nor do they have the other virtues required for their conversion and salvation."[15] However, these opinions were contrary to official Church and temporal policy.

The royal instruction of 1501 to Governor Nicolas Oviedo instructed the Spaniards to convert the Indians without the use of force: "Because we desire that the Indians be converted to our holy Catholic faith and that their souls be saved, for this is the greatest good that we can wish for, and because for this they must be informed of the matters of our faith, you are to take great care in ensuring that the clergy so inform them and admonish them with much love, and without using force, so that they may be converted as rapidly as possible."[16] The Laws of Burgos, promulgated in 1512, ordered the Spaniards to build churches for the Indians and to take pains to see that they were taught the Christian doctrine and their children were baptized. In 1520, Charles V and his council determined that "the Indians were free, ought to be treated as such, and induced to accept Christianity by the methods Christ had established."[17] Vasco de Quiroga, a judge of the *Audencia,* wrote in *Informacíon en derecho* (1535) that the Indians should be brought to the faith by persuasion and by "good and Christian influence, not by war and fear."[18] The advocacy of conversion to Christianity through good examples and appeals to reason remained, for the most part, an altruistic ideal that few followed. However, this policy may be related to the pattern of conversion that appears in the *Amadís Cycle.*

The conversion of pagans to Christianity appears in a number of Spanish romances of chivalry, but in no other work does it play such an important role. As John J. O'Connor has wryly noted, in the *Amadís Cycle* "the number of converted pagans is exceeded only by the thousands killed in myriad battles."[19] However, the attitudes displayed toward non-Christians differ markedly from book to book, depending on the author. Montalvo and Luján display a fierce animosity toward non-Christians, whereas Silva's depiction of his pagan characters is more tolerant.

In her study "Feliciano de Silva: A Sixteenth-Century Reader-Writer of Romance," Marie Cort Daniels contrasts the intense hatred for non-Christians apparent in Montalvo's text with Silva's tolerance.[20] Daniels notes how, in *Sergas de Esplandián,* Montalvo praises the Catholic Monarchs for their expulsion of the Moors from Granada: "They cast to the other side of the seas those infidels who, against all law and justice, had taken and held the kingdom of Granada for so many years. And . . . they cleaned it of that filthy leprosy, of that evil heresy that was spread throughout their kingdoms for many years."[21] Esplandián, the hero of *Sergas,* so intensely abhors all pagans that he discourteously refuses to greet Queen Calafia and her retinue when they first arrive in the Christian court, "because they were infidels, whom he mortally hated and desired to destroy."[22] Forced baptism, in which the hero promises to spare his enemy's life if the conquered will become a Christian, also appears in Montalvo's work as a valid means of winning converts to Christianity.

Luján displays a bitter antagonism toward non-Christians that is similar to Montalvo's. In *Silves de la Selva,* he calls the pagan forces "those unbelieving dogs that performed such deeds that they did not seem mortal men."[23] Like Montalvo, he presents forced baptism as a legitimate means of obtaining conversions. Lucendus, Silves's cousin, tells the giant Mondrago to convert to Christianity if he wishes to avoid a confrontation: "I want you to leave the evil adoration of your false gods and turn to the faith of our Lord Jesus Christ: and if you do this, I will be your friend . . . if not, I will engage you in battle."[24] When Mondrago refuses, Lucendus kills him.

As Daniels has observed, Silva pointedly criticizes such attitudes toward religious difference and conversion. Daniels notes that Silva's stance possibly reflects his own experiences with religious intolerance. His marriage to Gracia Fe, a New Christian of low social status, infuriated his relatives and caused serious problems for the couple's descendants. In addition, Silva's close friends were the leading *converso* writers of the day, Jorge de Montemayor and the exiled Núñez de Reinoso. It has even been argued that Silva himself was of *converso* descent.[25]

Silva eloquently expresses his condemnation of religious intolerance in *Florisel de Niquea,* part 4, book 1; his hero, Rogel de Grecia, criticizes Christians because they attempt to convert by force, rather than by example and sacrifice, as did Christ. Faith, he argues, must be accepted voluntarily: "Because faith, as something supernatural, is above all human reason, it is not lawful to make one believe its mysteries through force. . . . Faith must be voluntarily received, and the will cannot be constrained by any force, it must not be procured by force, indeed it should be admitted that no force is sufficient for [attaining] it, if the will, which is above all reason does not freely accept faith."[26] Daniels also points out how, in Silva's *Amadís de Grecia,* the hero, born a Christian but raised a pagan, asserts that an individual must choose faith through the exercise of reason, rather than because of custom or birth: "Whether or not my parents were Christian, it is in my hands to choose the best faith; for this is why the gods gave man reason to distinguish him among the beasts; he has free will to choose what is good, and to forsake what is not."[27] Even after he discovers his Christian background, Amadís refuses to convert, despite the urging of his father, Lisuarte, until he realizes for himself the truth of the Christian faith.

The previously noted animosity toward non-Christians that Montalvo displays in his text is notably lacking in his portrayal of Amazons. Silva, given his general tendencies toward tolerance, may be expected to portray pagan Amazons in a sympathetic light; however, Montalvo's treatment of the Amazon queen is completely out of character, given his usual presentation of non-Christians. In fact, Montalvo creates the pattern of Amazon conversion that Silva and Luján later follow in their texts: a pagan Amazon queen fights on the side of the infidels against the Christians and realizes the power and goodness of the Christian God through the example of the Christian knights; she freely decides to convert to Christianity, giving as her reason its inherent truth, and then fights with her former enemies, the Christians, against her former allies, the infidels.

Montalvo makes careful distinctions between the Amazon and other non-Christians, although the Amazon queen Calafia first appears in his text as a member of attacking pagan forces. In *Sergas de Esplandián,* Calafia does not join the pagan army because she wishes to destroy the Christians, as do the other infidels. In fact, she does not even know what a Christian is: "And hearing how most of the world was undertaking that voyage against the Christians, not knowing what a Christian was, nor having any knowledge of other lands but those that were her neighbors, wishing to see the world and its various peoples . . . she told all her subjects who were skilled in war that it would be good if, boarding their great fleet of ships, they set out on that voyage like those great princes and nobles."[28] Calafia merely wishes to see the world; her lack of malice and her complete ignorance of Christianity excuse her from Montalvo's general condemnation of all pagans. In fact, Montalvo's portrayal of Calafia's conversion mirrors those sentiments expressed in Silva's works: conversion can occur only through the exercise of reason, not through force.

41

In order to bring an end to the war between the pagan invaders and the Christian defenders of Constantinople, Calafia and the Grand Turk, the soldan of Liquia, challenge Amadís de Gaula and his son Esplandián to double combat. The outcome of their battle is to determine the victors of the war. Calafia battles Amadís, but even though she is a pagan, he refuses to attack her because of her sex. He fights defensively until he can capture her weapons without wounding her. She is then taken prisoner but treated with great honor.

Smitten by Esplandián's beauty and valor, Calafia at first decides to convert to Christianity to marry the young prince. Although her hopes are dashed by Esplandián's marriage to Leonorina, she decides to convert to Christianity anyway, giving as her reason the following: "Because as I have seen the just order of your law, and the great disorder of others, it is very clear that you follow the truth, and we, lies and falsehood."[29] The operative words in Calafia's conversion are *órden* (order), *verdad* (truth), and *conocimiento* (understanding), for they imply an acceptance of faith through understanding, thus showing that even this barbarian Amazon queen has come to embrace Christianity through the gentle persuasion of Amadís's good example and her own reason.

Esplandián, who lacks his father's courtly graces and diplomatic sense, has pointedly ignored the Amazon until this moment. Hearing her decision to convert, he joyfully embraces her and declares: "Queen Calafia, my good friend, until now you had not a word from me; because such is my nature that I cannot help but look upon those who are not in the holy law of the truth with anything but passionate enmity: but now that the most almighty Lord has done you this great mercy, of giving you such understanding that you have turned to his service, you will find in me great love, as if the King my father had engendered both of us."[30] Esplandián's acceptance of Calafia immediately following her decision to convert is an idealistic representation of the concept that all Christians are one in Christ. As such, it is bitterly ironic, given the racial hatred and persecution visited on converted Moors and Jews in sixteenth-century Spain.

To seal their friendship, Esplandián gives Calafia his cousin Talanque in marriage. Calafia's conversion involves the acceptance not only of Christianity but also of European cultural practices. She promises that her subjects will no longer engage in the Amazonian custom of living without men and of engaging in promiscuous sex with strangers but will follow the "normal habits of procreation between men and women."[31]

As Montalvo does with his characters, so is Luján careful to distinguish the Amazon from the other pagans of *Silves de la Selva*. As Montalvo does with Calafia, so does Luján reveal that the Amazon princess Pantasilea and her mother, Calpendra, do not join the pagan forces out of any malice held against the Christians or because they wish to destroy them. In fact, they are reluctant to fight against the Christians, a fact that Luján points out to his audience: "I want to make known to you that neither Queen Calpendra nor her beautiful daughter Pantasilea wanted to be involved in any of the above, because the war appeared unjust to them."[32] Pantasilea and Calpendra, like Calafia, come from a remote kingdom in the Indies; their distant geographical origin further distinguishes them from the other non-Christians, who come from eastern Europe and the Mediterranean.

The two Amazons visit Amadís de Gaula's court to request that Pantasilea be knighted by the illustrious king. Pantasilea and Amadís's illegitimate son Silves de la Selva immediately fall in love, and the two Amazons, completely won over by the Christians' kindness, graciousness, and chivalry, decide to leave their pagan comrades and join the Christian forces.

The distinction between the Amazons and the other non-Christians in Montalvo's and Luján's texts becomes less confusing after a look at the writings of many of the Indians' defenders. Although they advocate gentle persuasion and the use of reason in converting the Indians, these men show far less tolerance for Moors, Jews, or Turks. Although the Indians were not Christians, they had never rejected Christianity and therefore were not considered enemies of the faith, as were the Moors and Jews of reconquest Spain. Bartolomé de Las Casas, for example, carefully distinguishes between the Indians' nonbelief, which arose from ignorance, and the unbelief of Jews and Saracens, which he believed arose from stubbornness and malice:

> It is not the business of the Church to punish worshipers of idols because of their idolatry whenever it is not its business to punish unbelief, because the unbelief of Jews and Saracens is much more serious and damnable than the unbelief of idolaters. In the former, the definition of unbelief and the gravity of the sin are truly verified, whereas in the latter there is the obstacle of ignorance and deprivation in reference to hearing the word of God. . . . The Jews and the Saracens have heard the words of Christ, and the preaching of apostolic men and the words of gospel truth have daily beat against their hard hearts. But since they do not embrace the teaching of the gospel because of the previously mentioned pertinacity and insolence of their minds, they are guilty of a wicked malice. However, the worshipers of idols, at least in the case of the Indians . . . have never heard the teaching of Christian truth even through hearsay; so they sin less than the Jews or Saracens, for ignorance excuses to some small extent.[33]

Furthermore, Las Casas, like Sepúlveda, supported war against such infidels as the Turks, whom both believed maliciously impeded the spread of the gospel.[34] Obviously, the nonviolence that Las Casas advocated applied only to certain populations. Las Casas's *In Defense of the Indians,* like Montalvo's *Sergas de Esplandián* and Luján's *Silves de la Selva,* makes a marked distinction between those non-Christians who deserve tolerance and those who do not. Ignorance seems to be the major determinant, based on the notion that one cannot be held responsible for what one does not know.

The degree to which ignorance was held to determine the non-Christian's innocence of any religious wrongdoing was crucial to the debate concerning the Indians. Oviedo argued that they should be punished for having rejected Christianity because the faith had been brought to them centuries before Columbus. Oviedo based his outrageous assumption on a declaration by Pope Gregory the Great (590–604) that "the Holy Church has already preached the mystery of Redemption in all parts of the world."[35] Las Casas later argued the opposing view: "For who would judge that idolatrous Indians are to be punished when they had never, not even by hearsay, heard of Christ or Christians up to our own time and so are free from all guilt of malice?"[36]

The fictional Calafia, like the Indians of the New World, has no knowledge of Christians or Christianity before her contact with them. However, once she understands that the Christian religion is the one true faith, she converts; the Indians also willingly convert, according to their defenders, when they are brought to such an understanding through gentle persuasion and reason.

The hostility with which the sultans, Grand Turks, and caliphs of the *Amadís Cycle* are portrayed parallels the hostility that Las Casas and many like him demonstrated toward the non-Christians of the Old World: Indians were one issue, Saracens and Jews another. Although the authors of the *Amadís Cycle* seem to refer indiscriminately to non-Christians as pagans and infidels, a definite pattern of differentiation occurs. Those unbelievers who have no knowledge of or malice toward Christians, such as the Amazons, are treated with sympathy; those who resemble real-life threats to fifteenth- and sixteenth-century Europe—the Turks and Moors—are portrayed more harshly. Even Feliciano de Silva, who is more open-minded than Montalvo or Luján, shows far more tolerance toward such fantastical pagans as Amazons, giants, and the rulers of make-believe kingdoms than he does toward his Saracen characters.

In Silva's first addition to the *Amadís Cycle, Lisuarte de Grecia,* pagan forces again decide to attack Constantinople and destroy the Christians. As in *Sergas de Esplandián,* the war's outcome is to be decided through personal combat between the Christian and pagan leaders. Calafia fights at the side of Amadís de Gaula and the emperor of Trapisonda against the Amazon queen Pintiquinestra; king Armato, the leader of the entire pagan army;

and Grifilante, king of the Giant Islands. The two Amazons are so well matched that they fight for hours, with neither gaining the advantage. Calafia suggests that they rest and watch Amadís battle Grifilante. Pintiquinestra is so impressed by Amadís's valor that she decides to become a Christian. She tells Amadís: "Therefore, you will see that I will do the following, not out of fear, but because I esteem you. I will leave this battle and turn to your law; because you are the best knight in the world, and you could not be so without knowledge of the true faith."[37]

Pintiquinestra's decision to convert is an independent, rational action. She decides to join the Christian faith, not out of intimidation and fear, but through the exercise of her understanding. Amadís responds to her decision by kissing her hands and declaring "Whoever has thus come into understanding of the truth, well merits to have her hands kissed by kings."[38]

Although it is made very clear that Pintiquinestra's desire to convert to Christianity, like Calafia's, comes from an understanding of the "inherent truth" of the Christian religion, the political expediency of her decision to join the obviously more powerful Christian army adds a disquieting element to her conversion. Possibly, Silva meant to imply that conversion is not always a spiritual matter; after all, social and economic necessity compelled many New Christian conversions in Spain. Conversion brings Pintiquinestra many material benefits: she is joyfully welcomed into Amadís's court, baptized, given an illustrious Christian husband, and joins the winning side in its war against the infidels.

The motif of an Amazon queen's conversion to Christianity must have appealed greatly to Feliciano de Silva, for he employs it again in his two following texts, *Amadís de Grecia* and *Florisel de Niquea.* Although Silva closely imitated Montalvo in his depiction of Pintiquinestra's conversion, he fashioned the conversion of his two later Amazons, Zahara and her daughter, Alastraxerea, into an extended narrative dealing with the issues of humility versus arrogance and justice versus compassion. Only when Zahara has learned to control her great pride and Alastraxerea has learned that clemency must temper justice are the Amazons finally ready to accept the Christian faith.

Like the two earlier Amazon queens, Zahara, who first appears in *Amadís de Grecia,* arrives in Constantinople as a member of invading pagan forces. Zahara, however, seeks personal vengeance for the death of Zayr, the Sultan of Babilonia, whom she had planned to marry. She challenges Lisuarte, who killed Zayr in an earlier war, to individual combat. Like Calafia, she loses the battle to the Christian hero and is treated with great courtesy and kindness by the Christian court. At this point, her story diverges sharply from the earlier two. The proud Amazon refuses to become a Christian; nevertheless, she remains a good friend of the Christian princes, aiding them in battle and even saving Lisuarte's and Amadís de Grecia's lives on one occasion.

At the end of *Amadís de Grecia,* Zahara still has not converted. In fact, she has become an even more obdurate heathen because of a sexual encounter that she and Amadís de Grecia have had on a magic island. Because of the island's enchantment, neither the knight nor the Amazon has any recollection of their romantic encounter, although Zahara later finds herself pregnant. Genuinely confused by her condition, she prays to her idol, which tells her she has been impregnated by the god Mars: "The idol responded that because of her goodness and beauty, the great god Mars had fallen in love with her and had come to her in her sleep, and without her knowing, had relations with her. Therefore she should know that her womb was sacred and the child she gave birth to would be Mars'. For this she should give great thanks, because she now knew that the law of the gods would be increased by the child she bore."[39]

After giving birth to the twins Anaxartes and Alastraxerea, Zahara, believing herself to be a consort of the gods, demands that her subjects treat her as a divine being, approaching her on bended knee and prostrating themselves before her when they address her: "And she was laid in a rich bed: and from that point on she so highly esteemed herself that none of her queens nor anyone else dared to approach her but on their knees: and when they spoke to her they prostrated themselves on the ground as if before something sacred: for so she proclaimed she was, and the prince and princess [her children] were treated with the same reverence."[40]

When Zahara announces her divine offspring's birth to her Christian friends, Lisuarte's wife, Abra, a former pagan and ally of Zahara's, chastises the Amazon queen for her presumption and pride and urges her to convert to Christianity: "Consider royal princess that the debt we owe our sovereign Lord forbids us from consenting to the présumption committed by you against his divine majesty / as one who does not know his universal greatness and tribute / owed him by your sovereign gods / as god of gods / king of kings / and lord of lords / seeing that you lack this knowledge by living in an alien law."[41] Rather than feeling mortified at Abra's words, Zahara becomes enraged and continues to insist that she and her children are divine. The Amazon's refusal to accept Christianity at this point demonstrates Silva's repeatedly stated theme that conversion is an individual decision. The Amazon must choose faith through the exercise of her own reason and convert through her own volition.

In *Florisel de Niquea,* the brave and glorious deeds of Zahara's children, the Amazon Alastraxerea and her twin brother, Anaxartes, convince the pagan world that they are indeed divine: "Their fame extended quickly over the face of the earth: so that no one spoke of anything else: they were considered gods by the gentiles and esteemed and venerated wherever they were known."[42] The children of the god Mars and a "virgin" mother, they travel the world bringing justice to the oppressed and punishing wrongdoers. Silva presents the twins as Christ-like figures through the circumstances of their birth and their desire to bring a message of "good news" to people everywhere. However, whereas Christ preached humility, compassion, charity, and forgiveness, Alastraxerea and Anaxartes wield their swords to establish a "divine justice" based on strict and unforgiving standards of right and wrong.

Zahara and her children persist in believing themselves divine until circumstance forces the pagan queen to realize her error. Traveling with Amadís de Grecia, the Amazon returns to the enchanted island where her children were conceived, and the memory of her affair with Amadís returns to her as if in a dream. Only at this point does she become disabused of her notions of divinity and reject her gods: "She recollected the memory of all that had happened to her in that place / like a remembered dream all that had happened appeared to her: she felt a great shame for what she did and what had passed / and she began to say: O lying and false gods who with such deception allowed my chastity to be violated / believing my children to be divine and not human until now / in undeceiving me you have wished to show me the falsehood of your law."[43]

Zahara's inordinate pride in her children's divinity has become the source of her disgrace. Nevertheless, her experience has also taught her the Christian virtue of humility, and rather than cursing her fate, she realizes the opportunity now facing her. By accepting the Christian faith, she, her daughter, and her son become children of God. Furthermore, in gaining a heavenly father, the twins are reunited with their earthly one: "Although they [my children] lost a father, they gained the same / and in gaining him they achieve such glorious understanding that well it tempers the present pain: I wait for this with the understanding that my children's new father put in me of his holy Catholic faith. Wherefore my glorious children should obtain the understanding to leave being esteemed as children of false gods / and truly be children of He alone who created all creation with infinite and great power."[44]

Like the conversions of Calafia and Pintiquinestra, Zahara's conversion to Christianity is a product of her understanding (*conocimiento*). Although she persists in unbelief through most of *Amadís de Grecia, Florisel de Niquea* part 1, and *Florisel de Niquea* part 2, when she sees her error, her reasoning powers lead her to "the truth." Alastraxerea and Anaxartes similarly become Christians once they realize that they have been living in deception. Amadís de Grecia publicly acknowledges them as members of his own family, even though the twins have engaged in a particularly bloody war against their father. On the morning of Corpus Christi, "with great solemnity Queen Zahara and her children received baptism with such devotion that it was an admirable thing to see."[45] Furthermore, Alastraxerea gives up her Amazon identity by handing her sword to her father and asking him to choose a husband for her. Her newly discovered status as the illegitimate daughter of Amadís de Grecia and her conversion to Christianity signify her assimilation into European culture.

The conversion of the Amazons in the *Amadís Cycle* expresses an idealized conception of the proper relationship between the barbarian "other" and the subject of Western discourse, the white European male. Through the persuasion of patience, good example, and reason, these barbarian queens give up not only their religion but also their culture: they embrace and submit to the patriarchal institutions of Church and patrilineal monogamy. Such was the ideal to which aspired both the defenders of the Indians, such as Bartolomé de Las Casas, and the papal and Spanish royal policymakers. They believed that, on hearing the Gospel and seeing the good example of those who brought God's word, the Indians would readily give up not only their idolatry but also their cultural practices and embrace Christianity and European civilization. According to this logic, the only good Indian, like the only good Amazon, was a converted one.

NOTES

1. Herodotus, *History,* trans. A. D. Godley, Loeb Classical Library (Cambridge: Harvard University Press, 1957), 4: 116–17.

2. Strabo, *Geography,* trans. Horace Leonard Jones, Loeb Classical Library (Cambridge: Harvard University Press, 1969), 4:5.1–3.

3. C. H. Oldfather, trans., *Diodorus Siculus,* Loeb Classical Library (Cambridge: Harvard University Press, 1961), 3:55.3.

4. Cecil Jane, ed. and trans., *The Voyages of Christopher Columbus* (London: Argonaut Press, 1930), 263.

5. " . . . toda poblada de mujeres, sin varón ninguno, y que en cierto tiempo van de la tierra firme hombres, con los cuales han aceso, y las que quedan preñadas, si paren mujeres las guardan, y si hombres los echan de su compañía: y esta isla está diez jornadas desta provincia . . . Dicenme asimismo que es muy rica de perlas y oro" (quoted in "Cuarta Carta—Relación de Hernán Cortés al Emperador Carlos V, Tenoxtitlán, 15 de Octubre de 1524" in *Cartas y documentos,* introduction by Mario Hernandez Sanchez-Barba [Mexico: Editorial Porrua, 1963], 213).

6. Irving Leonard, *Books of the Brave* (Cambridge: Harvard University Press, 1949), 45–46.

7. Ibid., 51.

8. Ibid., 59.

9. Sydney P. Cravens, *Feliciano de Silva y los antecedentes de la novela pastoril en sus*

libros de caballerías, Estudios de Hispánofila 38 (Chapel Hill: University of North Carolina Press, 1976), 25.

10. Garci Rodríguez de Montalvo, *Sergas de Esplandián,* in *Libros de Caballeriás,* ed. Pascual de Gayangos, Biblioteca de Autores Españoles, 40 vols. (Madrid: 1857), 40:157, 539.

11. Feliciano de Silva is the author of *Amadís de Grecia* (Cuenca, 1530) and *Florisel de Niquea* (Valladolid, 1532).

12. Lewis Hanke, for example, in *Aristotle and the American Indians* (Chicago: Henry Regnery Co., 1959), 51, points out that "the Spaniards . . . made in America their first acquaintance with a matrilineal society. The queens and princesses they met both titillated them and scandalized their sense of propriety. The mores of a society in which the males did not make the rules were different from their own, and as 'civilized' persons have done around the world, they unhesitatingly condemned the unfamiliar culture pattern and proceeded to break it down."

13. Robert F. Berkhofer, *The White Man's Indian* (New York: Vintage Books, 1978), 8–10.

14. As quoted by Tzvetan Todorov in *The Conquest of America: The Question of the Other,* trans. Richard Howard (New York: Harper and Row, 1984), 151.

15. As quoted in Lewis Hanke, *All Mankind Is One* (DeKalb: Northern Illinois University Press, 1974), 11.

16. Ibid., 8.

17. Ibid., 11.

18. Ibid., 16.

19. John J. O'Connor, *"Amadís de Gaule" and Its Influence on Elizabethan Literature* (New Brunswick: Rutgers University Press, 1970), 123.

20. Marie Cort Daniels, "Feliciano de Silva: A Sixteenth-Century Reader-Writer of Romance," in *Creation and Re-creation: Experiments in Literary Form in Early Modern Spain,* ed. Ronald E. Surtz and Nora Weinerth (Newark, Del.: Juan de la Cuesta Hispanic Monographs, 1983), 83–85.

21. " . . . echaron del otro cabo de las mares aquellos infieles que tantos años el reino de Granada tomado y usurpado, contra toda ley y justicia tuvieron. Y . . . limpiaron de aquella sucia lepra, de aquella malvada herejia que en sus reinos sembrada por muchos años estaba" (Montalvo, *Sergas,* 505).

22. " . . . por ser infieles, á quien él mortalmente desamaba y habia voluntad de destruir" (ibid., 547).

23. " . . . aquellos perros descreydos [que] hazian cosas que no parecian hombres mortales" (Pedro de Luján, *Silves de la Selva* [Seville, 1549], 43, 45v.).

24. "Lo que quiero dixo Lucendus es que dexes la mala adoracion de tus muy falsos Dioses / tornandote a la fe de Jesu Christo nuestro señor: y haziendolo assi yo te sere buen amigo . . . si no comigo eres en batalla" (ibid., 58, 128v.).

25. Daniels, "Feliciano de Silva," 81. Constance Hubbard Rose discusses Silva's relationship to the *converso* community and the possibility of his own *converso* lineage in *Alonso Nuñez de Reinoso: The Lament of a Sixteenth-Century Exile* (Rutherford: Fairleigh Dickinson University Press, 1971), 28–35, 37.

26. " . . . la fe, como cosa sobrenatural, sobre toda razon humana, no es licito por

fuerça hazer creer sus misterios . . . voluntariamente se a de recebir, y la voluntad de ninguna fuerça pueda ser constreñida, no se a de procurar con la fuerça, hasta ser admitido lo que no basta para ello ninguna fuerça, si la voluntad libremente no recibe la fe que esta sobre toda razon" (Feliciano de Silva, *Florisel de Niquea* part 4, book 1 [Zaragoza, 1568], 80, 114r.).

27. " . . . si mis padres fueron Christianos, o que no lo sean, en mi mano es tener la ley que mejor fuere, que por esso tiene el hombre diferencia entre las bestias con la razon que los dioses en el puseron, pues para escoger lo bueno, y dexar lo no tal tiene libre albedrio" (Feliciano de Silva, *Amadís de Grecia* [Burgos, 1935], 9, 14v.).

28. "Y oyendo decir cómo toda la mayor parte del mundo se movia en aquel viaje contra los cristianos, no sabiendo qué cosa era Cristianos, ni teniendo noticia de otras tierras, sino aquellas que sus vecinas estaban, deseando ver el mundo y sus diversas generaciones . . . habló con todas aquellas que en guerra diestras estaban, que seria bueno que, entrando en sus muy grandes flotas, siguiesen aquel viaje que aquellos grandes prín*cipes* y altos hombres seguian" (Montalvo, *Sergas*, 540).

29. " . . . porque como yo haya visto la órden tan ordenada desta vuestra ley, y la gran desórden de las otras, muy claro se muestra ser por vosotros seguida la verdad, y por nosotros la mentira y falsedad" (ibid., 555).

30. "Reina Calafia, mi buena amiga, hasta aquí nunca de mí ninguna habla ni razon hubiste; porque es tal mi condicion, que si no son aquellos que en la ley santa de la verdad están y quieren bien á todos los otros que fuera della son, no puedo acabar comigo que mis ojos los miren sino con sañosa enemiga: ahora que el Señor muy poderoso esta tan gran merced te hace, de te dar tal conocimiento que su sierva te tornes, agora hallarás en mí grande amor, como si el Rey mi padre entrambos nos engendrara" (ibid.).

31. " . . . aquella isla mudará el estilo que de muy grandes tiempos hasta ahora ha guardado, por donde la natural generacion de los hombres y mujeres sucederán adelante" (ibid.).

32. "Pero tanto os hago saber que la reyna calpendra ni su hermosa hija pantasilea jamas en nada de los passado se quisieron hallar por paracerles injusta la guerra" (Luján, *Silves*, 44, 46r.).

33. Bartolomé de Las Casas, *In Defense of the Indians,* trans. and ed. Stafford Poole, C.M. (DeKalb: Northern Illinois University Press, 1974), 78.

34. Hanke, *All Mankind,* 91.

35. Ibid., 41.

36. Las Casas, *Defense,* 147.

37. " . . . por tanto veras que lo que te quiero decir mas por lo que te precio que por temor hare lo que de mi agora oyras: haziendo tu lo que yo te pidiere. Y es que yo dexare esta batalla y me tornare a tu ley: porque eres el mejor cavallero del mundo/el qual no pudiera estar ni bivir sino en el conocimiento verdadero" (Feliciano de Silva, *Lisuarte de Grecia* [Seville: 1525], 42, 42v.).

38. " . . . quien assi ha venido en conocimiento de la verdad/bien merece que reyes le besen las manos" (ibid., 42, 40v.).

39. " . . . el ydolo respondió que le hazia saber que por su gran bondad y hermosura el soberano dios Mares se auia della enamorado y que auia venido a

ella en sueños sin lo sentir y que auia tenido parte conella por do supiesse que el vientre que tenia era sagrado y lo que pariesse seria del dios Mares: porlo qual le diesse grandes gracia porque le hazia saber que la ley delos dioses seria acrecentada por lo que pariesse" (Silva, *Amadís de Grecia,* [Burgas] 127, 228v.).

40. "...y ella fue echada en un rico lecho: y tenia tanta presumpcion y estimada de ay adelante que ninguna reyna delas suyas ni otra persona ante ella osaua estar sino de hinojos: y quando le hablauan postradas por tierra como a cosa consagrada: que ansi lo publicaua ella estar y con el mismo acatamiento los infantes eran tratados" (Silva, *Florisel de Niquea* part 1 [Valladolid, 1532], 1, 1v.).

41. "Mira real princesa que no consiente la deuda que aquel soberano señor somos obligados a consentir tal soberuia contra su diuina magestad por ti cometida /como quien no conosce la su general grandeza y tributo/por los tus soberanos dioses a el deuido/como a dios de dioses/rey de reyes/y señor de señores. Y ya que este conocimiento por viuir en el ley estraña te faltara" (ibid., 1, 2r.).

42. "...muy presto su fama se estendio por todas las hazes de la tierra: tanto que en otra cosa no se hablada: tenidos entre los gentiles y estimados y acatados do eran conoscidos como a dioses" (ibid., 5, 9v.).

43. "...en todo su acuerdo y con memoria delo que por ella auia en aquella lugar passado/que como de sueño recordase le parescia todo auer passado: la qual grant verquenza de si tenia de lo que hecho y passado auia/que como sin sentido de auer passado lo que a su honestidad deuia fuera de aquel qu su marido fuesse/assi comiença a dezir. O engañosos y falsos dioses que con tanto engaño permitistes que mi limpieza violada fuesse/teniendo los mis soberanos hijos por diuinales y no humanos hasta agora que en desengañar me en engaño de vuestra ley me aues querido mostrar" (ibid., part 2, 53, 232r.).

44. "...por el padre que dexaron tal lo ganaron/qual de ganarlo sentiran perderlo/que con ganarlo pudieron cobrar la gloria de tal conoscimiento bien fue que se templasse con la pena presente: lo qual espero yo en aquel con el conoscimiento de nuevo padre de mis hijos me puso de su santa fe catholica lo querra remediar/donde los mis gloriosos hijos el tal conoscimiento deven tener en tanto quanto de salir de ser estimados por hijos de dioses de burla/y serlo de aquel solo que todo lo que criado pesce crio y hizo con infinito y sumo poder" (ibid., 53, 232r.).

45. "...con gran solemnidad la reyna zahara y sus hijos fueron baptizados con tanta devocion que cosa admirable de ver era" (ibid., 55, 236r.).

Amazonian Tyranny: Spenser's Radigund and Diachronic Mimesis

SUSANNE WOODS

Spenser's Radigund, the Amazon queen of book 5 of *The Faerie Queene*, gets a bad press. T. K. Dunseath refers to her as "unnatural Radigund," Jane Aptekar wittily calls her rule "the monstrous regiment of a woman," and Angus Fletcher sees Britomart, in the Temple of Isis, as learning to purge the Radigund in herself, "the masculine, violent, inequitable aspect of her . . . Amazonian nature."[1] And no wonder. Spenser himself apparently was not too kind to her. Alfred Gough, writing in 1918 and therefore considerably more sympathetic to the idea of women's equality than some more recent writers, summarizes Spenser's portrait: "In accordance with his general ethical scheme, the poet makes Radigund a symbol of what is in his eyes a form of injustice, the usurpation of authority by women. . . . Though not lacking in a certain wild grace, as of a tigress, [she] is depicted as treacherous, vindictive, cruel, and subject to fits of uncontrolled rage."[2]

Traditional Radigund portraits such as these anticipated a more recent tendency in Spenser studies to change Spenser from an idealizer of women, and especially of his queen, into a conflicted, power-loving, even violent personality who has a love-hate, sycophant-rebel reaction to that queen.[3] To some Spenserians, these newer trends appear a distortion, perhaps part of a current fascination with the alienated and deformed in society and literature, but in any case promoting ignorance of the Renaissance context and injustice to derivable authorial intention.[4] At the same time, Spenserians increasingly have come to agree that literature and its interpretation are political activities, whatever else they may be, and that we inevitably overlay our own ideas on Renaissance values. We should therefore be self-aware in our critical enterprise. Feminist scholars have also noticed, however, that rereadings of the Renaissance that privilege male power are often applauded, whereas those that suggest less misogynistic rereadings are likely to be attacked.[5]

With these trends and problems in mind, I want to look at the Radigund episode from a diachronic perspective, Renaissance and modern. I believe we can get a richer view of Radigund by juxtaposing points of view from then and now. For example, what do purportedly nonfictive Renaissance texts suggest about Amazons that might be relevant to Spenser's portrayal? Next, what do I see in the episode that a sixteenth-century reader might not have been able to articulate? In presenting the second perspective, I mean to be equally contextual and to deconstruct what is apparently, as opposed to what may be theoretically, in the actual language Spenser wrote.

Spenser understood *The Faerie Queene* to be mimetic as well as a "darke conceit," and like Sidney he creates a "second nature" based solidly on what his culture believed to be the first. The care he takes with geographies and genealogies shows the mimetic impulse—the attempt to establish in place and time a world of recognizable, as well as marvelous, reality. For him, as for his friend and patron, Sir Walter Ralegh, Amazons really existed, though in such questionable time and space as to provide excellent material for imaginative reconstruction.[6] The Portuguese explorer Francisco Lopes, for example, reported engaging with Amazon warriors in his 1542 travels down the river that now bears their name, an incident Ralegh cites in his 1614 *History of the World,* and Ralegh himself claimed to have heard firsthand accounts of contemporary Amazons during his 1595 travels to Guiana. These accounts, which Ralegh may well have conveyed to Spenser before the 1596 publication of the six books of *The Faerie Queene,* fit nicely with recent arguments that Spenser used reports of the New World to help situate and describe his Faery Land.[7]

Whatever the nature of Spenser's allegory in the Radigund episode— and I grant that it is richly political, social, and psychological—Spenser is also offering an imaginative representation of figures believed really to exist in his own time and to have existed in previous times. Further, though Amazons were creatures of fascinating danger for Renaissance writers, they were also historical figures of mixed connotation, as Ralegh's even-handed *History of the World* description attests. Shakespeare's Hippolyta in *A Midsummer Night's Dream* illustrates that, properly tamed, Amazons could even be graceful, queenly heroines.

Spenser's Renaissance reader, therefore, would probably approach an Amazon character with trepidation and a sense of the exotic, though not necessarily with fear and loathing. In book 5 of *The Faerie Queene,* Radigund is without question a dangerous threat to the social order, as well as more particularly a threat to Artegall, his mission, and his marriage with Britomart. Spenser paints her in some unflattering ways so that she may be a foil for Artegall's thematic significance (as a figure representing justice), a device for revealing his weakness, and a foil for Britomart's true queenliness. But she is on a different level of being from Spenser's allegorical horrors and magic ladies, such as Atin or Acrasia. Like Britomart and Artegall, she is an imaginative version of a perceived historical reality, even though she is not, like Arthur or St. George, an imaginative re-creation of what was widely believed to be a real, historical character. Unlike Britomart or Artegall, of course, Radigund is a version of bad reality.

Our late twentieth-century perspective allows us to see something about Radigund's badness that Spenser's readers may have perceived but not found easy to state directly, given their cultural assumptions about gender roles: Spenser presents Radigund as a victim, and as someone who must use indirection and the power of her sexuality to find authority in a cruel world of male power. The result of that need for indirection is perversion not only in the ordinary social scheme of things but also in a broader moral and ethical arena.

Amazonian tyranny comes from Radigund's need to use her girlish wiles instead of direct action, in which she has apparently been scorned and humiliated. Yet Spenser seems to blame the victim for the crimes committed against her and, by extension, against all women whom men have treated badly in love or politics. In Artegall's role reversal (spinning and weaving and wearing women's clothes), he becomes not merely a figure of humiliation but a patient Griselda accepting the justice of his fate—a victim who knows how to take the blame, as women then were routinely expected to do for their own misfortune, and as rape victims still are pressured to do today.

Artegall first hears of Radigund from Sir Terpin, another wandering knight, who describes how she has learned to hate men from her cruel treatment by Bellodant. A. C. Hamilton notes that "Bellodant" may mean "given to war . . . rather than to love; or giving war . . . , as he does when he rejects her." The name also may express Radigund's love of the profession of arms, closed to her though she tries "by all the waies she could" to enter it.[8] Sir Terpin tells Artegall that he would not have believed Radigund's martial prowess if he had not been directly overthrown himself. His description of her expresses admiration as well as amazement:

> Her name (quoth he) they **Radigund** doe call,
> A Princesse of great powre, and greater pride,
> And Queene of Amazons, in armes well tride,
> And sundry battels, which she hath atchieved
> With great successe, that her hath glorifide,
> And made her famous, more then is believed;
> Ne would I have it ween'd, had I not late it prieved. (5.4.33)

There is not hatred or fear in Sir Terpin's description so much as there is a man's complex admiration for and hostility toward a strong woman.

Beginning here and continuing throughout the episode, Spenser does not treat Radigund with the distaste Gough and Fletcher attribute to him, nor is he entirely unsympathetic to her victimization, as Dunseath and Aptekar imply. Instead, Spenser presents a complex character who provokes sympathy in female readers and fascination in male ones. She is an interesting victim whose plight continues to mirror realities we recognize.

Three key episodes offer glimpses of Radigund as mimetic of the interesting victim—a character with resonance in the post-Petrarchan world of Renaissance England and in the post-Freudian world of our own time. Those episodes are her actual fight with Artegall, her attempt to use Clarinda as a go-between in love, and her fight with Britomart.

The fight with Artegall is set up for Radigund to lose. She cannot control her passions, is in fact tyrannized by them, and assaults Artegall in fits of wild rage. Artegall knows perfectly well that such a wild attack wastes energy, and he waits for her to weaken, skillfully warding off her blows. She may have martial skills, but she is a terrible tactician. Yet she wins, not because of her skill, but because of her beauty.

The critical focus on this episode is usually on Artegall's folly, not Radigund's predicament.[9] What is an honorable appreciation of beauty in Artegall's similar encounter with Britomart in book 4 is dishonorable in book 5, but it is not altogether clear why. The reason, it seems to me, is that Artegall's attraction to Radigund is not merely sexual but a response to some latent virtue as well. If Radigund's beauty were not deeper than mere appearance, it would not have the effect it does. It is the *absence* of paint on her face ("voide of ornament," 5.5.12) that lets her beauty shine through. Artegall sees past the sweat and blood on Radigund's face to "the signes of feature excellent: / Like as the Moone in foggie winters night, / Doth seeme to be her selfe, though darkned be her light" (5.5.12). But he is already betrothed and has other business to do. Britomart's first reaction on hearing from Talus that Artegall is imprisoned and has been unfaithful to her is more true than critics have allowed.

Like the moon, Radigund is a Diana figure, but fogged and wintered. A conventional reading would assume that it is inappropriate and uncharacteristic for women to engage in battle, and battle brings the blood and sweat that fog true beauty. But the moon simile also works past the assumption of conventional gender roles to point to an acceptable warlike woman: Diana, the image of Queen Elizabeth, figured positively in Belphoebe and Britomart. Critics have suggested a negative glance at Queen Elizabeth in this passage, but no one, so far as I know, has suggested that it is a sympathetic portrayal of Radigund. Her innate virtue, like her beauty, has been perverted, but not by battle. That would render the portraits of Britomart and Belphoebe contradictory even for Spenser. Instead, Radigund's rejection by Bellodant and, by extension, the male world, clouds her face and makes her fierce.

Her injustice and tyranny are simply the flip side of what she has endured. If her tyranny expresses itself in the humiliation of Artegall, as commentators have generally assumed, it cannot escape a modern reader, and I doubt it entirely escaped Spenser's contemporaries, that the humiliating horror to which Artegall's loss reduces him is simply what women do every day.

Artegall ends up in women's clothes, doing women's work, because he is subject to Radigund's beauty. Radigund, for her part, prompts that subjection by the display she gives before the battle. The charm of her emissaries, sent the night before with food and drink, and her own magnificence garbed for the fight reflect women's wiles. Those wiles are not seen in the direct encounter of battle but in the indirect weakening of masculine intention that men always fear from women.

Radigund sends Artegall gifts before their battle that are meant to enervate him with sumptuous display. Ordering her envoy, Clarinda, to take the challenge to him, Radigund tells her to bring "to witnesse it, / Six of thy fellowes of the best array, / And beare with you both wine and iuncates fit, / And bid him eate, henceforth he oft shall hungry sit" (5.5.49). The combination of challenge and enticement characterizes the guile that, as Aptekar notes, "was considered to be the nature of all women."[10]

Similarly, Radigund's gorgeous battle array is conscious artistry. Whereas Artegall is simply the well-dressed combatant, Radigund has a style of her own:

> These noble warriors, mindefull to pursew
> The last daies purpose of their vowed fight,
> Them selves thereto preparde in order dew;
> The Knight, as best was seeming for a Knight,
> And th'Amazon, as best it likt her selfe to dight. (5.5.1)

And she likes to dress herself very grandly indeed:

> All in Camis light of purple silke
> Woven uppon with silver, subtly wrought,
> And quilted uppon sattin white as milke,
> Trayled with ribbands diversly distraught
> Like as a workmans hand their courses taught;
> Which was short tucked for light motion
> Up to her ham, but when she list, it raught
> Down to her lowest heele, and theruppon
> She wore for defense a mayled habergeon. (5.5.2)

This description, one of the more lavish in *The Faerie Queene*, goes on to detail her leg and thigh wear, her belt, and her shield, with its glorious portrait of a full moon:

> And on her shoulder hung her shield, bedeckt
> Uppon the bosse with stones, that shined wide,
> As the fair Moone in her most full aspect,
> That to the Moone it mote be like in each respect. (5.5.3)

Although many of these details have seductive overtones, they are so bound up with images of power and martial skill, with stately beauty, indeed with Queen Elizabeth (through the moon reference), that Radigund cannot be compared easily with such Spenserian seductresses as Duessa, Phaedria, Acrasia, Malecasta, or Hellnore. On the other hand, like Britomart, she is a warrior, though unlike Britomart her beauty is an essential part of her armor. After the moon on Radigund's shield is symbolically halved and then destroyed by her male antagonist, it is the show of thigh, the display of grandeur, the sheer beauty of presentation that combine to work their effect on Artegall, who sees the moon he has destroyed on her shield reappear in Radigund's face.

The indirect conquest effected by her beauty is turned against Radigund in the later episode of her lovesickness for Artegall. Unwilling or unable to confront him directly with the issue, she again sends Clarinda, this time with disastrous results. Radigund recognizes that her rule over Artegall is tyrannous; she is moved by him personally, and seeks a way both to free him and to keep him bound to her:

> Bound unto me, but not with such hard bands
> Of strong compulsion, and streight violence,
> As now in miserable state he stands;
> But with sweet love and sure benevolence,
> Voide of malitious mind, or foule offence. (5.5.33)

Radigund's apparent nobility of spirit is undercut by her unwillingness or inability to approach Artegall directly. She continues with an appeal to Clarinda:

> To which if thou canst win him any way,
> Without discoverie of my thoughts pretence,
> Both goodly meede of him it purchase may,
> And eke with gratefull service me right well apay. (5.5.33)

Clarinda, of course, falls for Artegall herself and, caught in a web of passion and deception, lies to them both. She presents Artegall's gracious response to Radigund's initial inquiry as if he had rejected her out of hand, and Radigund's persistent entreaties to Artegall as if she were becoming increasingly cruel. The perverse tragedy of this story may be measured by comparing it to the famous go-between story of American lore: John Smith's wooing of Priscilla on behalf of Miles Standish. John speaks for

Miles, who wants Priscilla to know how he feels but is too shy to speak; Priscilla falls for the messenger, who honorably steps away from her affection until released from his position by Miles. Everything is direct and honorable and ends happily, except maybe for Miles, who at least has the contentment of his own virtue. The Miles Standish story is a boy's story about manly virtues; the Radigund story is a girl's story about a woman who has been victimized in love and whose resulting perverse and indirect behavior creates even more pain for herself and those she might care about.

Ultimately, the victim must die, which Radigund does in battle with a woman of privilege who has not had, or caused, the pain Radigund has. Britomart is her father's heir, her lover's beloved, and an exceptional woman who is given permission to act in a man's world. The fight between Radigund and Britomart is ostensibly a fight over right rule, with Radigund protecting her kingdom and Britomart determined to return it to male rule. This apparently direct confrontation has a not very submerged subtext, however. As Britomart fights to save Artegall and all the other men, she is actually asserting her sexual supremacy over another attractive woman:

> The trumpets sound, and they together run
> With greedy rage, and with their faulchins smot;
> Ne either sought the others strokes to shun,
> But through great fury both their skill forgot,
> And practicke use in armes; ne spared not
> Their dainty parts, which nature had created
> So faire and tender, without staine or spot,
> For other uses, then they them translated;
> Which they now hackt and hewd, as if such use they hated. (5.7.29)

They fight until the grass is "fild with bloud," which Spenser takes care to make a clear symbol for their sexuality:

> all in gore
> They trode, and on the ground their lives did strow,
> Like fruitles seede, of which untimely death should grow. (5.7.31)

The combatants taunt each other over Artegall, and the fight gets even fiercer. Britomart finally repairs Artegall's mistake by slaying the beautiful Amazon, but Britomart's reasons are complex and the act itself problematic. Having stunned Radigund,

> the wrothfull Britonesse
> Stayd not, till she came to her self againe,
> But in revenge both of her loves distresse,
> And her late vile reproch, though vaunted vaine,
> And also of her wound, which sore did paine,
> She with one stroke did head and helmet cleft,

> Which dreadfull sight, when all her warlike train
> There present saw, each one of sence bereft,
> Fled fast into the towne, and her sole victor left. (5.7.34)

In conquering Radigund, the unusually barbaric Britomart has conquered all other women.

This is a typical male fantasy of female competition for men, but I think there is more to it. The glamour and lovesickness Spenser describes for Radigund, the recognition he gives her of her unfairness to Artegall, and, most particularly, the power of language he attributes to her combine to create a remarkably sympathetic portrait. Some of this sympathy may suggest that Spenser himself might have had reason to identify with Radigund.

Like the ambitious Amazon, Spenser must be indirect and use display to present power. Like a woman, a poet must weave and spin, not take direct action against those whom he would challenge. Spenser's technique for conquest, like Radigund's, is less direct and straightforward than it at first appears. Throughout book 5, it seems to me, he subverts his own message of masculine privilege, from the sympathetic features of the Radigund portrait to the ironic use of Britomart to restore masculine rule to the Amazons.[11] He himself was the victim of powerful displeasure from Lord Burghley, an experience that might have extended itself to some comprehension of the powerlessness of women and more certainly to considerable understanding of the power of beauty and of skillful indirect speech and action. Their dangers he also acknowledges, sadly, even tragically, in the story of Radigund.

Radigund's bad press is justified only by a narrow view of Spenser's intention and a credulous acceptance of the sterner dicta of Renaissance misogyny. Although she is unquestionably portrayed in strong negative language as a tyranness emblematic of improper and perverse rule, she is also mimetic of a more sympathetic reality on at least three levels: she has the stately mystery believed to be true of real Amazons; she enacts a tragedy of female powerlessness that we can deconstruct in our time, one that probably was not totally inaccessible to Spenser; and the dilemma of Radigund's scorned beauty is the poet's own.

Radigund is also a figure whose predicament and dangerousness are mimetic of political and social realities that appear vastly different across time—that is, she presents a successful diachronic mimesis. In the context of the imaginative second nature of Spenser's Faery Land, she can touch the frontiers of social and cultural awareness in the twentieth century as she doubtless did, though in a somewhat different way, in the sixteenth. The genius to create such characters, perpetually marveled at in Shakespeare, is more common in Spenser than I believe we have yet realized, distracted as we usually have been by the richness of allegorical structures in *The Faerie Queene*. Recognizing an author's subtle characterizing power, such as Spenser's in the Radigund episode, has implications for many of our ongoing critical debates, including the relation of literary to other texts, the nature of intertextuality, and the role of the reader in determining significance and value in literary discourse.

It is time to look anew at some old ideas. We might start with mimesis.

NOTES

1. T. K. Dunseath, *Spenser's Allegory of Justice in Book V of "The Faerie Queene"* (Princeton: Princeton University Press, 1968), 5; Jane Aptekar, *Icons of Justice: Iconography and Thematic Imagery in Book V of "The Faerie Queene"* (New York: Columbia University Press, 1968), 23; Angus Fletcher, *The Prophetic Moment: An Essay on Spenser* (Chicago: University of Chicago Press, 1971), 279.

2. Alfred E. Gough, "Commentary," in Edmund Spenser, *The Faerie Queene, Book V,* ed. Alfred E. Gough (Oxford: Oxford University Press, 1918), 207.

3. Contrast William Nelson, *The Poetry of Edmund Spenser* (New York: Columbia University Press, 1963), and Thomas P. Roche, *The Kindly Flame* (Princeton: Princeton University Press, 1964), with Stephen Greenblatt's chapter on Spenser in *Renaissance Self-fashioning* (Chicago: University of Chicago Press, 1980) and Louis Adrian Montrose, "The Elizabethan Subject and the Spenserian Text," in *Literary Theory/Renaissance Texts,* ed. Patricia Parker and David Quint (Baltimore: Johns Hopkins University Press, 1980), 303–40.

4. For valuable examples of the recent fascination with studies of Renaissance deformity and transgression, see Peter Stallybrass and Allon White, *The Politics and Poetics of Transgression* (Ithaca: Cornell University Press, 1986), and Marjorie Garber, ed., *Cannibals, Witches, and Divorce: Estranging the Renaissance,* Selected Papers from the English Institute, 1985, n.s. 11 (Baltimore: Johns Hopkins University Press, 1987).

5. A recent and fairly typical engagement occurred at session 182 of the 22nd International Congress on Medieval Studies, held at Kalamazoo, where Mary A. Pryor in her talk, "Artegall's Marriage Nightmare," argued that the Radigund episode in book 5 of *The Faerie Queene* undercuts hierarchical notions of marriage and is subversive rather than supportive of strict patriarchal notions of rule. In a mostly appreciative response, John N. Webster disagreed, preferring to see the episode in a more conventionally thematic terms (*Spenser Newsletter* 18 [1987]: 47).

6. Ralegh devotes two folio pages of *The History of the World* (London, 1614) to argue that "Amazons have beene, and are" (4.2.15, Rrrr2–Rrrr2v).

7. Ralegh, *The Discoverie of the Large, Rich, and Bewtiful Empyre of Guiana* (London, 1596), D4–D4v. On Spenser's use of the New World, see Michael Murrin, "Spenser's Fairyland," in *The Allegorical Epic: Essays in Its Rise and Decline* (Chicago: University of Chicago Press, 1980), 131–52, and John N. Wall, Jr., " 'Fruitfullest Virginia': Edmund Spenser, Roanoke Island, and the Bower of Bliss," *Renaissance Papers* (1985): 1–17.

8. A. C. Hamilton, ed., *The Faerie Queene* by Edmund Spenser (London: Longman's, 1977), 554; *Faerie Queene* 5.4.30. Texts cited in the essay are from this edition.

9. Typical is Kathleen Williams, *Spenser's World of Glass: A Reading of "The Faerie Queene"* (Berkeley: University of California Press, 1966), 171: "There is no doubt of Artegall's blame in this encounter. He is well aware of his own shame as he had earlier been of Terpin's, and the poet's defense of him is perfectly managed, persuading us to contemplate his weakness."

10. Aptekar, *Icons,* 132.

11. Susanne Woods, "Spenser and the Problem of Women's Rule," *Huntington Library Quarterly* 48 (Spring 1985): 141–58.

Amazons and Aristocrats:
The Function of Pyrocles'
Amazon Role in Sidney's
Revised *Arcadia*

MARGARET M. SULLIVAN

Critical discussion of Pyrocles' Amazon costume in the *Arcadia*s has focused most often on the question of whether it is "good" or "bad" for a man to disguise himself as a woman. Assessment of the device remains divided, as it must when literary interpretation employs moral terms. Some critics consider Pyrocles' disguise to be a good, or "masculine," strategy because his beloved's father forbids her the company of men; others are convinced that his Amazon garb signifies authorial disapproval of the prince's bad, or "effeminate," infatuation with Philoclea.[1] The function of Pyrocles' Amazon disguise—the focus of this essay—has received little attention, perhaps because it is perceived as obvious.[2] I will argue that questions about the basis of male property rights to women, which arise during the trial scene in book 5 of the *Old Arcadia,* help to explain the services that Pyrocles-Zelmane performs for the princesses only in the *New Arcadia.* Both texts dramatize the analogical relation between monarchy and patriarchy, but only the revised text subjects its male Amazon to the same gender code that paralyzes Basilius's daughters. Pyrocles' frustrated attempts to assert his martial prowess while disguised as a woman reveal the extent to which socially imposed gender restrictions create the feminine weakness they posit as natural. The revised text, though apparently headed toward another version of the *Old Arcadia*'s marital denouement, breaks off in midsentence; through the figures of Pamela and Philoclea, the new material of book 3 makes claims for female autonomy that threaten a social hierarchy based—with the problematically public exception of Elizabeth Tudor—on male property rights to women.

To understand the function of the Amazon hero in the *New Arcadia,* it is necessary to outline contradictions left unresolved in the *Old.* Victor Skretkowicz's careful reconstruction of the text's history suggests (despite the critical utility of distinguishing between an "old," or finished, and a

"new," or fragmentary, *Arcadia*) that if constant revision of the same manuscript is any indication of authorial intention, Sidney considered neither
work complete. As Skretkowicz puts it, "strictly speaking, Sidney's principal
source [for the *New Arcadia*] is his *Old Arcadia,* of which Greville regarded
this second version as a 'correction'."[3] By removing the entr'acte eclogues
from the *Old Arcadia,* Sidney "corrected" the text's apparent endorsement,
effected through structural irony, of the patriarchal family as a model for
the hierarchical state.[4] The original book 3, for example, narrates the
various plots by which the major characters attempt to escape the confines
of the family; these aristocratic antics are judged lacking when juxtaposed
with the shepherds' orderly patriarchal community. As Musidorus contem-
plates assaulting the sleeping Pamela and Philoclea consummates her love
for Pyrocles, the narrator breaks off to follow the pastoral pipe to a wedding
in which Lalus, a shepherd, marries Kala, a shepherdess, "with consent of
both parents," a blessing "without which neither Lalus would ask" for her
hand "nor Kala grant" it (*OA,* 244).

In the Third Eclogues, which celebrate Kala and Lalus's wedding, the
fear that female sexuality might not be firmly and justly within full masculine control is raised only to be dismissed. After Dicus confidently concludes the couple's epithalamium with the assertion that "Hymen *will* their
coupled joys maintain" (*OA,* 248, my emphasis), another shepherd, Nico,
sings a bawdy fabliau about a husband whose jealousy provokes his wife
into taking a lover. The disruptive specter of unlicensed female sexuality
Nico conjures up is quickly laid to rest in the verse marriage manual that
follows it. Pas, disturbed that Nico "hath picked out such a tale, with
intention to keep a husband from jealousy, which were enough to make a
sanctified husband jealous, to see subtleties so much in the feminine
gender," rejects the disconcerting idea that male control of female sexuality
ultimately depends on female consent (*OA,* 253). He answers Nico with
"Who Doth Desire That Chaste His Wife Should Be," a poem that puts the
responsibility for women's chastity back into men's hands by asserting that
good husbands guarantee faithful wives (*OA,* 253–54). And though Pas's
poem is followed by Philisides' indecorous beast fable about the origins of
monarchy, "As I My Little Flock on Ister Bank" (*OA,* 254–59), the eclogues
close on a reassuring note with a debate between the wise old patriarch
Geron and a young, misogynistic shepherd named Histor.[5] Geron's paean
of marriage, "In Faith, Good Histor, Long Is Your Delay," disguises the
relation between tyranny in the state and tyranny in the family hinted at in
the placement of "Ister Bank" (*OA,* 260–64). Geron denies the comparison
between the two forms of hierarchy by insisting that men and women have
separate but equal roles, the former in the public domain and the latter in
private, male-owned domains: "I have a wife worthy to be a queen, / So well

she can command, and yet obey; / In ruling of a house so well she's seen" (*OA,* 262). Geron's "separate but equal" argument seems convincing, at least to the all-male audience of shepherds, whose economic and emotional needs it serves: "As we to get are framed, so they to spare; / We made for pains, our pains they made to cherish; / We care abroad, and they of home have care" (*OA,* 263). But the pseudoequality asserted by Arcadia's pastors is not endorsed by their Grecian masters.

King Euarchus, who acts as judge in the trial that closes book 5 of the *Old Arcadia,* explicitly links the foundation of civilization to inequality; each of his rulings stresses the necessity of keeping property—in which category he includes (rather like a proto–Lévi-Strauss) wives and daughters—in the hands of male elders. When Euarchus condemns Gynecia to death, he does so in dual terms; the duchess is sentenced both as Basilius's wife and as an Arcadian subject. As a self-confessed husband-murderer, Gynecia threatens society precisely because her crime denies the metaphysical underpinnings of marriage, an institution that Euarchus calls "the most *holy* conjunction that falls to mankind, out of which all families, and so consequently all societies, do proceed" (*OA,* 383, my emphasis). Euarchus attempts to extend the category of mankind to include women by claiming that Gynecia must die "for the due satisfaction to eternal justice and accomplishment of the Arcadian statutes" (*OA,* 383). Yet the judge distinguishes between men, who are property-owning political subjects, and wives, who are subject to their husbands, when he orders Gynecia's execution as an "everlasting example to all wives *and* subjects" (*OA,* 383, my emphasis). All wives are subject to their husbands, despite Geron's assertion of his wife's equality. After having been provoked into a false confession by a guilty conscience (like former president Jimmy Carter, Gynecia has lusted in her heart), the duchess is condemned to death; her fate warns women that no station is exempt from the hierarchy of gender. Her execution as a regicide, on the other hand, serves as a warning to another group, the group of political subjects that includes Geron but excludes both his wife and the duchess.

That daughters belong to their fathers just as wives belong to their husbands becomes apparent when Euarchus sentences Pyrocles and Musidorus, who, being men, are held responsible for the actions of Basilius's daughters. Pyrocles falsely claims that he attempted but failed to rape Philoclea. He is sentenced to be thrown from a tower because, according to Euarchus, "nothing can be imagined more unnatural than by force to take that which, being holily used, is the root of humanity [and] the beginning and maintaining of living creatures, whereof the confusion must needs be a general ruin" (*OA,* 405–6). Euarchus worries about the confusion of ownership rights—to children, as well as to other forms of property—that would occur if the Arcadians were to allow unlicensed sexuality on the part of women.[6] Musidorus is judged guilty of both private and public property theft. Euarchus treats the prince's private theft (i.e., eloping with Pamela) as harshly as Pyrocles' attempt to rape Philoclea because the judge considers both princesses to be their father's property. "Although [Musidorus] ravished [Pamela] not from herself," Euarchus declares, "yet he ravished her from him that ow[n]ed her, which was her father" (*OA*, 406). Musidorus's public theft consists of having eloped with Basilius's eldest daughter and heir, an act that Euarchus compares to the abduction of Helen, with the rather obvious implication that Arcadia, like Troy, would be destroyed if it were to condone such goings on: "And although Helen was a wife and this but a child, that booteth not, since the principal cause of marrying wives is that *we* may have children of our own" (*OA*, 406, my emphasis). Euarchus's "we" refers, quite literally, to patriarchs, and it grammatically unites his hereditary position as the king of a country (who stands in for Arcadia's Duke Basilius) with the position of any father in any family.

In modern terms, Pyrocles is sentenced for breaking and entering; Musidorus, for attempting to cross Greek city-state lines with stolen property. When Pyrocles and Musidorus point out that they have exchanged promises to marry with the princesses (who, unlike most forms of property, have the power of speech), Euarchus dismisses the consent of Pamela and Philoclea as irrelevant:

> For if the governors of justice shall take such a scope as to measure the foot of the law by a show of conveniency, and [to] measure that conveniency not by the public society but by that which is fittest for them which offend, [it follows that] young men, strong men, and rich men shall ever find private conveniences how to palliate such committed disorders as to the public shall not only be inconvenient but pestilent. The marriage perchance might be fit for them [i.e., for the princesses and princes], but very unfit were it to the state to allow a pattern of such procurations of marriage. (*OA*, 407)

The "state" in question is both the marital state, which protects the property rights of fathers and husbands, and "the public society" based on the power that a hierarchical government, at least analogically, grants to those same men. Sons and nephews, it seems, have neither political power nor the property rights to women that such power signifies—unless, of course, they inherit or otherwise acquire property and become husbands and fathers themselves.

Throughout the trial, the princesses are made conspicuous by their absence. Philanax, a deputy governor who turns prosecuting attorney after the supposed death of Duke Basilius, claims that he keeps Pamela and Philoclea secluded because "neither wisdom would [that] they should be brought in presence of the people, which might thereupon grow to new uproars, nor justice required [that] they should be drawn to any shame, till somebody accused them" (*OA,* 375). The second motive for sparing the princesses seems hollow, because Philanax's supposed chivalry allows the silenced Philoclea to be condemned without a trial. Euarchus sentences the younger princess—apparently on the unverbalized charge of "suspected sexual activity"—to life imprisonment in a community of vestal nuns, "so to repay the touched honour of her house with well observing a strict profession of chastity" (*OA,* 381).

A difference between Pamela and Philoclea that cuts across gender categories makes the elder princess's absence essential to Sidney's denouement. When Philanax further justifies his reasons for sequestering both of Basilius's daughters, he reminds his auditors that "as for Pamela . . . the laws of Arcadia would not allow any judgement of her, although she herself were to determine nothing till age or marriage enabled her" (*OA,* 375). As women, Pamela and Philoclea are not considered responsible for their actions. The judge assumes that a daughter belongs to her father until given in marriage to another man, at which time legal responsibility for the daughter-turned-wife passes into the hands of her husband. Basilius had not authorized such a transfer; hence, in Euarchus's judgment, the princes are no better than thieves. But Pamela's status as heir to her father's power contradicts the very basis on which Philoclea is sentenced: it seems all women are property *except* those who are patrilineally privileged in lieu of male heirs. Pamela is positioned not only above the laws that Euarchus invokes to sentence Pyrocles and Musidorus but also outside the restricted feminine code to which Euarchus subjects Gynecia (the untrustworthy wife) and Philoclea (the disobedient daughter).

The *Old Arcadia* providentially dispels the contradictions of Pamela's status; the same "eternal justice" that Euarchus invokes while sentencing Gynecia for the murder of her husband saves face for a patriarchal government in the nick of time. Before Euarchus's unjust sentences can be carried out, the crowd sees Basilius move; startled, "some [of them] began to fear spirits, some to look for a miracle, most to imagine they knew not what" (*OA,* 415). The duke's "miraculous" resurrection has left many of Sidney's readers uncomfortable; judging from his revisions, he himself was none too happy with it. For one thing, the duke's "death" conveniently directs the reader's attention away from his own sins against the patriarchal family. Whereas Gynecia's desire for Pyrocles is represented in anguished soliloquies that uphold the "holy conjunction" of matrimonial monogamy, her husband happily pursues a liaison with Cleophila. Even if the duchess (who inadvertently induced her husband's deathlike trance with a love potion) *had* been guilty of manslaughter, Euarchus's sentence would still be an ironic comment on the definition of marriage that he uses to justify her execution: "the most holy conjunction that falls to *man*kind" (*OA*, 383, my emphasis). The duchess is suicidally guilty over the accidental "death" of a husband who, though not made the instrument of hastening her death, nevertheless has been calmly looking forward to it throughout the narrative. A prediction that he would commit adultery with his wife "most rejoiced" Basilius, because he "interpreted the meaning thereof that he should accomplish his unlawful desires with Cleophila, and that after (by the death of Gynecia) she should become his wife" (*OA*, 133).[7]

The duchess's plight certainly undermines the justice invoked in book 5. Yet the narrative makes the absence of the princesses (whose letters the reader, if not Euarchus, has read) felt even more strongly than the presence of Gynecia. On Basilius's death, the duchess becomes a spokesperson for both gender and state hierarchies. Gynecia is the sole woman permitted to speak in book 5's public trial because she uses the opportunity to support patriarchy and condemn herself. By contrast, the "humble-hearted" Philoclea speaks only in "a private petition," a letter that Philanax witholds even after Euarchus sentences her to solitary confinement for life (*OA*, 396). Pyrocles and Philoclea are, of course, innocent of Basilius's murder. The narrative puts its readers in the position of either agreeing that a daughter is a piece of property, in which case Philoclea deserves her sentence for having "stolen" herself from her father, or finding Euarchus's sentence unjust. The judge's verdict upholds male rights to confer (in Basilius's case, to withhold) sexual access to female kin. The problem Sidney's contemporary readers faced is that the same rights supported the social hierarchy of Elizabethan England. The royally arrogant tone of Pamela's letter to the court is a discomforting reminder of how difficult it was for Elizabeth Tudor's subjects to uphold the power of a female monarch while representing as natural the subordination of other women. Pamela's letter, juxtaposed with that of her sister, expresses her difference in kind, not only from the text's other female characters, but also from the subjects it addresses: "To whom to write, where may I learn, since yet I wot not how to entitle you? Shall I call you my sovereigns? Set down your laws that I may do you homage. Shall I fall lower, and name you my fellows? Show me, I beseech you, the lord and master over us. But shall Basilius's heir name herself your princess? Alas, I am your prisoner" (*OA*, 397).

The difficulty with trying to represent a gender hierarchy within an aristocratic one is that a woman like Pamela, distinguished from women per se by primogenitural inheritance of royal blood, cannot be represented as inferior to men per se with any consistency. In the words of anthropologist Sherry Ortner, "the logic of hierarchical systems inherently tends toward (even if it never reaches) gender equality. At any given level in the system, men's and women's statuses are more similar to one another's than to persons of either sex at other levels."[8] The text's endorsement of patrilineal primogeniture explains why Pamela cannot be allowed to speak at the trial: Euarchus's legal proceedings would constitute a form of rebellion were they conducted against the express wishes of the duke's successor. The only two characters whose power runs parallel to Pamela's are Euarchus (de jure ruler of Macedonia, but only a visiting adjudicator in Arcadia) and Musidorus, who is, as Pyrocles reminds his father, de jure ruler of Thessalia, though his mother is acting as regent while the princes make their grand tour (*OA,* 414). The princesses speak only by letter so that a patriarchal presence can save face for a patrilineal system that has been radically undermined by its own contradictions. The revisions that resulted in the *New Arcadia* are attempts to resolve these contradictions, and it seems reasonable to assume that the attempts were prompted by Sidney's own experience of the relations between gender and power in England under Elizabeth Tudor.[9] Pamela most resembles England's queen during the period when she believes her father is dead; ironically addressing her letter to "sovereigns" and "fellows," she accuses her subjects of rebellion.[10] But Euarchus ignores Pamela's patrilineal authority and bases his verdict on her subordinate place within the patriarchal family. The massive revisions indicate that Sidney was aware of the contradictions inherent in differentiating between Geron's domesticated "queen of the house" and a female heir who, like Queen Elizabeth, might rightfully rule the men who claimed a right to rule women and children within the patriarchal family.

Sidney's unusually strong pride in his matrilineal heritage explains the *Old Arcadia*'s contradictory attitude toward gender; the text conveys more sympathy toward the social position of women than Elizabeth Tudor ever expressed, at least in the historical record. The queen's right to rule was based on her patrilineal inheritance of royal blood, and she was not likely to jeopardize it by promoting equality for anyone. For most of his life, Sidney's contact with his ruler was filtered through his maternal uncle, the earl of Leicester, who was Elizabeth's favorite. From his attendance at the famous Kenilworth Festivities in 1575 to his post under Leicester at Zutphen in 1585, Sidney was reminded constantly that any power held by his uncle totally depended on the queen's affections.[11] So did Dudley's properties, a point Elizabeth wittily emphasized in responding to his courtly compliments at Kenilworth. When reassured by "the Lady of this pleasant lake," one of Leicester's hired players, that "Lake, Lodge" and "Lord" were still hers to command, the queen replied: "We had thought the lake had been ours, and do you call it yours, now? Well, we will herein commune more with you hereafter."[12] This firsthand knowledge of the way *all* masculine power, in an England ruled by Elizabeth I, rested on a feminine basis was reinforced by Sidney's own anomalous position as heir apparent to his uncles' patrimonies by virtue of his mother's Dudley blood.

Katherine Duncan-Jones introduces the *Defence of Leicester,* the document in which Sidney lauds his Dudley genealogy, by deprecating its value as "mainly historical." She considers the text another in a series of efforts made by Elizabeth's new men "to demonstrate, often by gross distortions of the evidence, that those who had most political power were also those of most ancient nobility" and points out that "Leicester's claim to nobility" was weak because "every important connection [came] from the female line" (*MP,* 126). Without denying Duncan-Jones's statement that "contemporary heralds would almost certainly have given" this matrilineal "objection . . . some weight" (*MP,* 127), as a twentieth-century critic I hesitate to endorse their point of view. Sidney is, of course, indirectly boasting of his own noble blood by praising Dudley, and the earl's title was bestowed by the queen rather than inherited. But Leicester's great-grandmother "*was* a Talbot," and his grandmother "*was* a right Gray, and a sole inheritrix of that Gray" (*MP,* 134–35, my emphasis). To call the claims Sidney makes on the basis of that lineage "very plausible" is to accept, somewhat paradoxically, the weight of patrilineal nobility and the weakness of matrilineal nobility. Distaste for what Duncan-Jones calls the text's "unattractiveness" is understandable, given that in the twentieth-century the dominant ideology professes equality. But Duncan-Jones's speculations about whether the *Defence of Leicester* was spurred on by the death of Dudley's young son (the heir whose birth had blighted Sidney's great expectations) seem sordid only if we ignore the contradictions of our own society, in which "equality" signifies private ownership of, and inherited access to, property. And shying away from the concept of inherently noble blood prevents us from noticing the assertion in the *Defence of Leicester* that such superiority can be matrilineally based. To preserve for himself (perhaps even more than for his uncle) the fiction of a hereditary right to high position in the Elizabethan social hierarchy, Sidney calls an equally fictional gender hierarchy into question.

The Defence of Leicester stresses the same biological fact that so many parents emphasize today by hyphenating the surnames of their progeny: children are a joint project. Admittedly, this matrilineal consciousness has its limits; just as when children's names are hyphenated today, the father's is usually the *last* last name, so too Sidney's "right Gray" was married to Edmund Dudley and consequently the mother of John Dudley, not John Gray. But by insisting that a woman retains her natal identity rather than agreeing with the notion that on marriage it is lost or submerged in the family of her husband, Sidney calls into question the distinction on which gender hierarchy is based. *The Defence of Leicester* openly professes a matrilineal pride that renders problematic its male speaker's patronymic identity.

Although admitting that his father, Henry Sidney, is "of ancient and always well esteemed and well matched gentry," Philip Sidney claims that his matrilineal heritage is primary: "I do acknowledge, I say, that my chiefest honour is to be a Dudley, and truly am glad to have cause to set forth the nobility of that blood whereof I am descended" (*MP,* 134).[13] Behind this assertion lies another: though Mary Dudley Sidney, as the female sibling of male heirs, could claim the Dudley patrimonies only through her son, she nevertheless retained her possession of noble Dudley blood and her right to the prestige that was conferred on the nobility in Elizabethan England.[14]

Sidney's desire to explore both the basis of male property rights to women and the limits on those rights led to the revisions that became the *New Arcadia.* I do not suggest that the birth of Leicester's son early in 1581—the son who supplanted Sidney as heir to the Dudley patrimonies—bears any direct causal relationship to the revised text.[15] But according to Jean Robertson, the bulk of the *Old Arcadia,* a work that seems a good deal more comfortable with the hierarchies that be than does the *New,* was completed between March and August 1580, a period when Sidney still had hopes of inheriting the Dudley estates (*OA,* xvi). Robertson also suggests that, on finishing the work in 1581, the unsatisfied author continued to "tinker" with it a year or so before beginning the extensive rewriting that produced the *New Arcadia* (*OA,* xvii). Victor Skretkowicz estimates that the revisions ended around 1584, so that the changes were produced during a period when the disinherited Sidney might well have been ambivalent about patriarchal justice (*NA,* xiv). At the very least, enough of his identity was involved in proving the nobility of Dudley blood for him to take on contemporary heralds by asserting that female ancestors were capable of transmitting aristocratic prestige to their descendents, property or no. In short, Sidney seems to have accepted—albeit with a certain amount of ironic anxiety—the principle that hierarchies of blood cut across the hierarchy of gender.[16]

But the plots of both *Arcadia*s revolve around courtship. And marriage, as Gayle Rubin points out, depends on the cultural construction of different kinds of human beings: "Kinship systems rest upon marriage. They therefore transform males and females into 'men' and 'women,' each an incomplete half which can only find wholeness when united with the other."[17] One significant gendered difference that Sidney retains in the *New Arcadia* is the restriction to men of effective force, the ability to engage in mortal combat. In the *Old Arcadia,* Pyrocles' Amazon disguise fulfilled the same purpose that its prototype did in *Amadís de Gaule:* it enabled the hero to gain access to a princess whose father had forbidden her the company of men.[18] Again as in *Amadís,* the use of this disguise in the *Old Arcadia* is primarily comic, involving the hero in various sexual contretemps with his beloved, her mother, and her father. Descriptive passages and added episodes in the *New Arcadia* turn the Amazon costume into a vehicle for exploring the cultural construction of both femininity and masculinity. In both *Arcadia*s Pyrocles asserts that women, given the same enculturation, could equal the martial exploits of men: "And, for example, even this estate of [the] Amazon's, which I now for my greatest honour do seek to counterfeit, doth well witness that, if generally the sweetness of their disposition did not make them see the vainness of these things which we account glorious, [women] neither want valour of mind, nor yet doth their fairness take away their force" (*OA*, 21; cf. the minor changes in *NA*, 73). But in the *New Arcadia*, both the first description that we get of Pyrocles (*NA*, 7–8)[19] and, later, the reaction of Kalander's household to the androgynous prince (who has exhibited his martial prowess under the masculine assumed identity of "Daiphantus") emphasize the instability of gender categories: [Daiphantus] "being now well-viewed to have no hair of his face to witness him a man, who had done acts beyond the degree of a man . . . to have a Mars' heart in a Cupid's body, all that beheld him (and all that might behold him did behold him) made their eyes quick messengers to their minds that there they had seen the uttermost that in mankind might be seen" (*NA*, 42). The *New Arcadia* exploits the image of the Amazon by rendering the myth of a matriarchal state full of women warriors as if it were possible, but it does so only through Pyrocles, the "uttermost that in *man*kind might be seen."[20]

Because he was revising toward the *Old Arcadia*'s denouement,[21] Sidney needed to maintain a form of difference that would gender his characters. If Pamela and Philoclea were not dependent on Musidorus and Pyrocles, it would be difficult to justify their subordination within a marital hierarchy. A successful female warrior would unbalance the gender economy of the text; Pyrocles-Zelmane's role is to preserve the princesses from the effects of masculine violence and, as an Amazon who is really a man, to ensure a feminine dependence that makes sense of marriage. In three episodes added to the *New Arcadia*, the Amazon steps in when the princesses' property rights to themselves are threatened by violence. Zelmane acts for the princesses, who have been enculturated to passivity, at those points in the narrative when only martial training can prevent the loss (real or symbolic) of the princesses' rights to their own persons, which rights are presented as being over and above their father's paternal right to withhold those persons. Pamela and Philoclea are endowed with the right to give themselves away *because* their father refuses to do so; Sidney's plot ensures that the princesses circulate despite Basilius's attempt to withold them from "the traffic in women."

The first new Amazon episode takes place during Phalantus's tourney. A "knight called Phebilus, a gentleman of that country," who has fallen in love with Philoclea, challenges Phalantus, loses in combat, and forfeits the princess's picture, much to her "modest discontentment" (*NA*, 100–101). Zelmane, who "had come upon the spur to redeem Philoclea's picture" because she "could not bear" to have it "in captivity, if the cunning she had learned in her country of the noble Amazons could withstand it," defeats Phalantus the following day and wins the picture back (*NA*, 104). In doing so, Zelmane wins praise for Amazonian, rather than Pyroclean, prowess and leaves the royal family "all thinking [that] they honoured themselves in honouring so accomplished a *person* as Zelmane" (*NA*, 104, my emphasis). Although it might seem disingenuous to call this episode a property dispute—after all, Phalantus has a picture to which Philoclea has no claim, not Philoclea herself—the princess's lack of control over her image parallels her lack of control over her person. Philoclea is present at the tourney only because Basilius fears that Zelmane the Amazon will depart, bored from the restrictions he has placed on his daughters, if she is not offered some form of spectacle (*NA*, 90). A woman who is also a free agent, Basilius realizes, must be amused; his captive daughter provides part of the entertainment.

The second episode in which Zelmane acts for Philoclea seems, on the surface, equally trivial. In what is also the reader's first encounter with Amphialus, Pyroclean jealousy over a new rival's admiration of Philoclea provokes Zelmane into wounding a man who refuses to defend himself. The "courteous Amphialus" will neither fight with Philoclea's female champion nor return the princess's glove, as Zelmane requests. Amphialus's adherence to the chivalric code explains both his desire to keep the glove and his refusal to fight with a woman; he politely asks Zelmane for "leave to keep" what his "heart cannot persuade itself to part from" (*NA*, 196). The fetishistic keeping of such a token, however, is not merely a chivalrous gesture. Amphialus repeats it later when, having gained possession of Philoclea herself,[22] he takes the princess's knives and wears them into combat, falsely indicating her favor (*NA*, 321). The seemingly harmless chivalry in the glove scene at the river Ladon prepares the reader for Amphialus's acceptance of his mother's kidnapping plot in book 3. Metonymically, possession of the token against Philoclea's will is equated with possession of Philoclea's person against her will, as the princess's reaction to the fight over her glove indicates: "Philoclea, that was even jealous of herself for Zelmane, would needs have her glove, and not without so mighty a lour as that face could yield" (*NA*, 198).

When it comes to women, possession seems to be nine-tenths of the law. First, Basilius locks up his daughters as if they were his private property; then, Amphialus, in defending his own decision to keep them locked up, asserts that Pamela and Philoclea are Arcadian public property (*NA*, 325). Neither of the two men considers the wishes of the women. Yet Basilius's action is upheld by a metaphysical sanction that Pamela herself invokes in refuting her aunt's atheistic scoffing at the notion of a father's right to prevent his daughter's marriage. "If he be peevish," Basilius's heir tells Cecropia, "yet is he my father; and how beautiful soever I be, I am his daughter, so as God claims at my hands obedience, and makes me no judge of his imperfections" (*NA*, 358). As Pamela's pious speech indicates, the revisions prompted by the trial scene at the end of book 5 of the *Old Arcadia* included the creation of princesses who were incapable of committing even the slightest misdemeanor. It is difficult to imagine Pamela eloping after having delivered that impassioned speech defending patriarchy. And Philoclea, who consummated her love at the first opportunity in the *Old Arcadia,* urges Pyrocles to virtuous restraint when a similar opportunity is offered in the *New* (*NA*, 233). Book 3, which focuses on the near-perfect princesses, seems designed to give Basilius's daughters an opportunity to earn the self-possession that Euarchus's property-based sentences denied them in the *Old Arcadia.* Both Pamela and Philoclea stand up to an extraordinary series of ordeals designed to pressure them into marrying their cousin, Amphialus, against their father's wishes. In overcoming everything from persuasive rhetoric (*NA*, 322–24, 329–35, 336–37, 354–63) to physical torture (*NA*, 419–23) to the psychological torture of death threats (*NA*, 424–27, 431–37), they defeat all the stereotypes of feminine frailty that were used to justify the subjection of women.[23]

For all their admirable qualities, however, the revised Pamela and Philoclea are not endowed with the ability to protect themselves. When the princesses and Zelmane initially are subjected to the "amorous" attentions of the braggart-bully Anaxius and his two brothers, the Amazon counsels stalling. In the end, Zelmane, who has not stood up at all well to an extended period of unarmed incarceration, must act to preserve the princesses because the plot "come[s] again to the strait she most feared for them, either of death or dishonour" (*NA*, 460). Having killed Anaxius's less skillful brothers, Zelmane is probably capable of defeating Anaxius as well (*NA*, 460–61); the Amazon gives a speech that seems to prepare the reader for "her" victory over a self-proclaimed misogynist shortly before the text breaks off. When Anaxius bewails the shameful fate that forces him to fight with a woman, Zelmane taunts him: "Thou doost well indeed," she says, "to impute thy case to the heavenly providence—which will have thy pride find itself, even in that whereof thou art most proud [i.e., martial ability], punished by the weak sex, which thou most contemnest" (*NA*, 465). But the episode breaks off in midsentence *before* Zelmane kills Anaxius, perhaps because the heavenly providence that the Amazon invokes also upholds Basilius's right to deny his daughters to the princes. In short, Sidney seems to have revised himself into a corner.

The excellent Philoclea and Pamela of the *New Arcadia* are incapable of an act of treason, which is what disobedience to one's father entails if one's father is a king. Yet Pamela, who bitterly protests Zelmane's council to string along Anaxius and his brothers in the hope of a rescue, seems to find death equal, if not preferable, to returning home: "Why should we delight to make ourselves any longer balls to injurious fortune? Since our own parents are content to be tyrants over us, since our own kin are content traitorously to abuse us, certainly, in mishap it may be some comfort to us that we are lighted in these fellows' hands, who yet will keep us from having cause of being miserable by our friends' means" (*NA*, 455).[24] What Pamela's protest points out is that the effect of her father's just authority—pastoral imprisonment in Arcadia—differs very little from that of the authority usurped by Cecropia and Amphialus, who incarcerate the princesses in their castle. The former locked them up to prevent them from marrying; the latter, to force them to marry. That the princesses might have a choice in the matter does not occur to their jailers. Pamela's desire to commit suicide expresses her frustration with a culture that does not grant a woman the authority to dispose of her person in any other way.

Pamela's status as heir to the throne further complicates matters, for to rebel against her father's authority calls the whole system of inherited power into question. If the excellence of the princesses is their own, an individual attribute rather than a property of birth, on what basis can the hereditary succession that puts an unworthy Basilius on the throne be justified? And if Basilius's rightful authority is to be upheld, on what basis can Pamela and Philoclea act against it? The defeat of Anaxius, which would return the princesses to their "rightful" owner, could not resolve the questions raised by Sidney's plot.

The *New Arcadia* answers the questions it raises about the basis of men's property rights to women in two ways. One answer, to judge by the activities Pyrocles-Zelmane performs for the princesses, is that a male-dominated society systematically denies martial training to women to create a physical weakness that lends credence to the metaphysics of gender difference.[25] The myth of the Amazon inverts the dominance/submission polarities of gender formation in a patriarchal culture, with one important difference: in the matriarchal state of the Amazons, the dominant gender, woman, does not marry; after mating to reproduce their kind, the women either kill or dismiss the men who have inseminated them. The Amazons' male children are sometimes killed at birth, sometimes sent to their fathers, and often crippled and forced to spin. Such variant forms of the myth attempt to explain the subordination of women in a patriarchal culture.[26] But the most significant difference between the two societies is the absence of marriage,[27] which prevents conflicting relations between genealogy and gender in the Amazonian state. In this particular form of matrilineal government, property consistently passes *through* women *to* women. In a patrilineal government, the power and property that pass through women occasionally get to a female heir. Like Pamela at the end of the *Old Arcadia* or Elizabeth Tudor during Sidney's lifetime, such a woman is a structural anomaly and an embarrassing contradiction to the natural hierarchy of gender.

Other than brute force, the only answer to the basis of male property rights to women that the *New Arcadia* offers is Pamela's metaphysical justification of Basilius's authority: "I am his daughter, so as God claims at my hands obedience, and makes me no judge of his imperfections" (*NA,* 358). This ambivalent representation of gender is not surprising, given the contradiction between Sidney's desire to claim his distaff inheritance of noble blood and his inability to renounce the privileges that patriarchy confers on men. The *New Arcadia* demonstrates the interdependence of the metaphysical notions that support hierarchy; in questioning the basis of male property rights to women, the text also calls into question the basis of hereditary property rights. When the democratic implications of his plot undermined the privileged status to which Sidney laid claim, he stopped writing. After all, in the country of the Amazons, Zelmane herself was an aristocrat, "niece to Senicia, queen thereof" and "lineally descended of the famous Penthesilea" (*NA,* 83).

A disinherited Philip Sidney who attempted, and failed, to revise into reconciliation the socially constructed hierarchies of blood and gender seems to me a more interesting historical figure than the "president of nobelesse and chivalrie" lauded by Spenser. The fragmentary *New Arcadia* raises questions that the polished *Old Arcadia* answered by silencing the princesses until a miraculously resurrected Basilius could bestow his bless-ings on a marital denouement that put Musidorus on the Arcadian throne.[28] Fictive questioning of hierarchy in Tudor England started with a trip to Utopia; Sidney's contribution to this interrogation ends in the middle of a duel in Arcadia. Thomas More could envision government without private property but not a state without the patriarchal family; Sidney could question the natural basis of gender but not a hierarchical state based on the inheritance of royal blood. *Utopia* and the *New Arcadia* are the textual pales beyond which sixteenth-century English humanism could not venture. What Sidney said about *Utopia* in the *Defence of Poetry* might well be applied to his own attempt to envision an autonomous woman within a hierarchical state. He saw the way to female autonomy but could not accept the means: "I say the way, because where Sir Thomas More erred, it was the fault of the *man* and not of the poet, for that way of patterning a common wealth was most absolute, though *he* perchance hath not so absolutely performed it" (*MP,* 86–87, my emphasis).

NOTES

1. The strongest anti-Amazon stance is taken by Mark Rose, who states his belief that Sidney "intended his readers to find Pyrocles' disguise offensive" in "Sidney's Womanish Man," *Review of English Studies* 15 (1964): 354. A more positive assessment of the disguise can be found in Margaret E. Dana, "Heroic and Pastoral: Sidney's *Arcadia* as Masquerade," *Comparative Literature* 25 (1973): 308–20; Elizabeth Dipple, "Metamorphosis in Sidney's *Arcadias*," *Philological Quarterly* 50 (1971): 47–62; and Josephine Roberts, "Herculean Love in Sir Philip Sidney's Two Versions of *Arcadia*," *Explorations in Renaissance Culture* 14 (1978): 43–54.

2. My decision to analyze the function of the Amazon disguise is indebted to Frederic Jameson's *Political Unconscious: Narrative as a Socially Symbolic Act* (Ithaca: Cornell University Press, 1981). I realized that a materialist analysis of Pyrocles-Zelmane would be a useful way to avoid essentializing gender after reading Jameson's comments on Heathcliff's function in Emily Brontë's *Wuthering Heights*. Jameson, albeit indirectly, demystifies the critical commonplace that the Brontës were unable to portray realistic masculine characters by asking his readers "to see Heathcliff as a historical modification of the donor," a function that "allows us to glimpse the *ideologeme*—the conceptual antinomy but also the social contradiction—which generates the narrative, but which it is the latter's mission to 'resolve' " (128). This note is not the place to point out the differences between a nineteenth-century narrative produced in a capitalist England and a sixteenth-century narrative produced in a semifeudal England. Those differences aside, I would argue that the *New Arcadia*'s Amazon disguise is an attempt to resolve the social contradiction between ranking human beings according to their possession of inherently superior blood and maintaining that women are innately inferior to men.

3. Victor Skretkowicz, "General Introduction," in Philip Sidney, *The Countess of Pembroke's Arcadia (The New Arcadia)*, ed. Victor Skretkowicz (Oxford: Oxford University Press, 1987), xvii; all further references to the *New Arcadia* will be to this edition and will be cited in the text as *NA*. For further discussion of textual issues, see William A. Ringler's edition of *The Poems of Sir Philip Sidney* (Oxford: Oxford University Press, 1962), 364–82; and Jean Robertson's introduction to Sidney's *Countess of Pembroke's Arcadia (The Old Arcadia)* (Oxford: Oxford University Press, 1973), xlii–lxxi. All references to the *Old Arcadia* will be to the Robertson edition, cited in the text as *OA*.

4. In "The Traffic in Women: Notes on the 'Political Economy' of Sex," in *Toward an Anthropology of Women*, ed. Rayna R. Reiter (New York: Monthly Review Press, 1975), 157–210, Gayle Rubin explains how gender construction within the patriarchal family reproduces a social system in which "men have certain rights in their female kin" whereas "women do not have the same rights either to themselves or to their male kin" (177). Those who know Rubin's ground-breaking essay will recognize its influence throughout my own.

5. For discussions of the political viewpoint of "Ister Bank," see Martin Raitiere, *Faire Bitts: Sir Philip Sidney and Renaissance Political Theory* (Pittsburgh: Duquesne University Press, 1984); and Annabel Patterson, " 'Under . . . Pretty Tales': Intention

in Sidney's *Arcadia,*" *Studies in the Literary Imagination* 15 (1982): 5–21. Geron's response to the poem—"he never saw [a] thing worse proportioned than to bring in a tale of he knew not what beasts at such a banquet when rather some song of love, or matter for joyful melody, was to be brought forth"—seems designed to move the reader to look for a connection between the paternalistic gender hierarchy praised in the shepherds' eclogues and Philisides' portrait of man the monarch, who first protects and then enslaves his beast-subjects in "Ister Bank" (*OA,* 259).

6. Age, as well as caste, cuts across gender categories; recall that the *Old Arcadia* was written by a young, unmarried aristocrat, a man who lived nearly all his life a dependent. A significantly different attitude toward gender emerges when male children grow into men with property rights to women and children of their own. For an interesting anthropological analysis of the temporary alliance (in hierarchical societies) between women and young men who lack property, see Melissa Llewelyn-Davies, "Women, Warriors, and Patriarchs," in *Sexual Meanings: The Cultural Construction of Gender and Sexuality,* ed. Sherry B. Ortner and Harriet Whitehead (Cambridge: Cambridge University Press, 1981), 330–58; compare Kenneth Rowe's remarks on the difference between Walter Ralegh's own youthful love match and the extremely pragmatic premarital advice he gave his son in *Romantic Love and Parental Authority in Sydney's* [*sic*] *"Arcadia,"* University of Michigan Contributions in Modern Philology, 24 vols. (Ann Arbor: University of Michigan Press, 1947), 4:1 50–51, 57.

7. Perhaps Basilius was counting on his wife's dying from natural causes, but it seems unlikely; Gynecia is described as "having passed five and thirty years of her age even to admiration of her beautiful body" (*OA,* 384), whereas the octogenarian duke is described as "an old broken vessel" (*OA,* 45).

8. Sherry B. Ortner, "Gender and Sexuality in Hierarchical Societies: The Case of Polynesia and Some Comparative Implications," in Ortner and Whitehead, eds., *Sexual Meanings,* 397. Ortner's analysis of Polynesia has "comparative implications" for most lineage-based societies, including feudal Europe (359). Although Sidney lived during a period in which many questioned the feudal notion that social status was fixed at birth, the *Arcadia*s endorse (theoretically permanent) lineal hierarchies.

9. Gayle Rubin defines gender as "a socially imposed division of the sexes" and "a product of the social relations of sexuality" (Rubin, "Traffic," 179). In early modern England, patrilineage could empower women despite "social relations of sexuality" that, more often than not, marginalized them. Elizabeth Tudor is the most obvious historical example of such empowerment; for an interesting discussion of how the queen manipulated the theoretical dichotomy between her "masculine" political power and her "feminine" body, see Allison Heisch, "Queen Elizabeth I: Parliamentary Rhetoric and the Exercise of Power," *Signs* 1 (1975): 31–55.

10. Although Pamela does not represent Elizabeth Tudor in any simple sense, her impresas in both *Arcadia*s do ask the reader to compare the princess with England's queen. Pamela's "perfect white lamb tied at a stake with a great number of chains, as it had been feared lest the silly creature should do some great harm" (*OA,* 37), recalls an image John Stubbs used to describe the queen in his anti-Alençon

pamphlet, *A Gaping Gulphe Wherein England Is Like to Be Swallowed*. Although historical hindsight leads some writers to claim that the queen's marriage negotiations were never serious, Stubbs's patriotism (or fear of the French and Catholicism) led him to interpret the match as a threat to both Elizabeth and England. Stubbs envisioned "the very foundation of our commonwealth dangerously digged at by the French, and our dear Queen Elizabeth (I shake to speak it) led blindfold as a poor lamb to the slaughter"; the *Gaping Gulphe* is quoted in Elizabeth Jenkins, *Elizabeth the Great* (New York: Coward-McCann, 1959), 226. A comparison between Pamela and Elizabeth is suggested even more strongly by the princess's jeweled impresa in the *New Arcadia*, a diamond with a "word" translating the queen's motto, *Semper eadem*, as "Yet still myself" (*NA*, 84). For evidence that Stubbs's pamphlet influenced Sidney's own contribution to the anti-Alençon campaign, the *Letter to Elizabeth*, see Katherine Duncan-Jones's introduction to the *Letter* in *Miscellaneous Prose of Sir Philip Sidney*, ed. Duncan-Jones and Jan van Dorsten (Oxford: Oxford University Press, 1973), 31–32; all further references to this edition will be cited parenthetically in the text as *MP*.

The most important difference between the two female rulers is age: Elizabeth Tudor was twenty-five when she became monarch; Pamela is seventeen when she is told of Basilius's death. Philanax justifies the princess's imprisonment by citing the "ancient laws of Arcadia," which bear a proviso that Pamela "was to have no sway of government till she came to one and twenty years of age, or were married" (*OA*, 319). "And married I am," Pamela assures him, "therefore I demand your due allegiance" (*OA*, 319). But Philanax, like Euarchus, refuses to recognize Pamela's right to give herself in marriage, thereby preventing Basilius's heir from assuming her rightful place in the seat of judgment.

11. On Kenilworth, see Malcolm Wallace, *The Life of Sir Philip Sidney* (Cambridge: Cambridge University Press, 1915), 153–56. Wallace relates that when Leicester accepted governorship of the states against Elizabeth's express orders, her fury took the form of reminding him that disobedience was especially heinous in "a man raised up by ourself, and extraordinarily favoured by us above any other subject of this land," and suggests that the queen's displeasure immediately undermined Leicester's (and consequently Sidney's) authority in the Netherlands, where "it was rumoured that Leicester was considered a poor creature even by the English Queen, who had never intended to prosecute the war seriously" (352).

12. Jenkins, *Elizabeth*, 198. However much Sidney disagreed with the queen on matters of policy, he probably appreciated the mastery of linguistic skills that enabled her to rule independently instead of relying on male intermediaries. Elizabeth's intellectual gifts, which were no small argument against the natural inferiority of women, are described by J. E. Neale in *Queen Elizabeth* (New York: Harcourt Brace, 1934). Neale notes that if Elizabeth had "not been a fine linguist, she would have been compelled to refer an extensive branch of statecraft—diplomatic relations—to her Council, for no foreign ambassador spoke English" (67). And though in 1561 Cecil might have prayed for a husband to control the queen—"God send our mistress a husband, and by time a son, that we may hope our posterity shall have a masculine succession" (Neale, *Elizabeth*, 103)—when Sidney wrote his

Letter to Elizabeth in 1579, court politics forced him to argue for Elizabeth's superior single status and against her subordination within a marital hierarchy.

13. Henry Sidney was proud of his hypergamous match. In *Penshurst: The Semiotics of Place and the Poetics of History* (Madison: University of Wisconsin Press, 1984), 102, Don E. Wayne notes that Henry displayed both Sidney and Dudley arms after his marriage to Mary Dudley, combining both in a screen that he added to the family estate, Penshurst. When Sidney wrote to the twelve-year-old Philip, who was enrolled at Shrewsbury School, he encouraged the boy's identification with his matrilineal kin: "Remember, my son, the noble blood you are descended of by your mother's side"; the letter is reprinted in James Osborn, *Young Philip Sidney: 1572–1577* (New Haven: Yale University Press, 1972), 13. As Osborn's collection of Sidney's continental correspondence makes clear, the prestige of being considered a Dudley in all but name remained an important part of Philip's identity; see, for example, Languet's letter introducing Philip to Dr. Johan von Glauburg (*Young Philip*, 297). Anthropologist Sherry Ortner points out that in traditional hierarchical societies "the father is seen as the fixed point of reference, while the mother acts as the variable, that is, all things being equal, one inherits one's father's rank or status, but if there are major divergences of status between mother and father in either direction, the mother exerts the greater pull on the child's status, up or down" (Ortner, "Gender," 365).

14. For a discussion of the difference between "prestige" and "property," see Sherry B. Ortner and Harriet Whitehead, "Introduction: Accounting for Sexual Meanings," *Sexual Meanings,* 13–21. Prestige and property often go together, but need not. Sidney's life is a nice example of the distinction made by Ortner and Whitehead: petitions and dedications testify to his prestige, but his frustrated attempts to win the queen's patronage testify to his poverty.

15. In "Sir Philip Sidney and the Matchmakers," *Modern Language Review* 33 (1938): 512, Denver Baughan points out that Sidney probably knew about Leicester's marriage to Lettice Knollys Devereux as early as 1577. Four years passed before Sidney received the shock of losing his place to Leicester's son. It seems reasonable to assume that he began to question gender hierarchy seriously only after losing his position as heir apparent.

16. The *Defence of Leicester*'s rapid tonal shifts—from boasting to belligerent to apologetic—indicate Sidney's anxiety about founding the Dudley claim to nobility on the distaff side of the family tree. He moves from a matrilineal claim that "the mother being an heir hath been in all ages and countries sufficient to nobilitate" her successors to the patrilineal complaint that his opponent, the anonymous author of *Leicester's Commonwealth,* has left the Dudleys "fatherless clean" (*MP,* 135, 138). For a discussion of possible relations between the *Defence of Leicester* and a new focus on genealogy in the Arcadian revisions, see Denver Baughan, "Sidney's *Defence of the Earl of Leicester* and the Revised *Arcadia,*" *Journal of English and Germanic Philology* 51 (1952): 34–41.

17. Rubin, "Traffic," 179.

18. For the parallels between *Amadís de Gaule* and Sidney's *Arcadia,* see John O'Connor, *"Amadís de Gaule" and Its Influence on Elizabethan Literature* (New Brunswick: Rutgers University Press, 1970), 183–201.

19. Dipple compares the *New Arcadia*'s opening description of an androgynous Pyrocles with its description of his Amazon disguise and concludes that "what had seemed comically feminine and sexual in the *Old Arcadia* is, through this contextual resonance, made martial and masculine" (Dipple, "Metamorphosis," 57).

20. For two surveys that stress the polysemy of the Amazon myth, see Celeste Turner-Wright, "The Amazons in Elizabethan Literature," *Studies in Philology* 37 (1940): 433–56; and Abby Wettan Kleinbaum, *The War against the Amazons* (New York: McGraw-Hill, 1983), 5–137.

21. We cannot know what form this marital denouement might have taken. But when Sidney revised the oracle that sent Basilus into pastoral retirement in the *Old Arcadia,* he added lines (italicized below) that prepare the reader for both the trial and the weddings:

> Thy elder care shall from thy careful face
> By princely mean by stol'n and yet not lost;
> Thy younger shall with nature's bliss embrace
> An uncouth love, which nature hateth most.
> *Both they themselves unto such two shall wed,*
> *Who at thy bier, as at a bar, shall plead*
> *Why thee (a living man) they had made dead.*
> In thy own seat a foreign state sit.
> And ere that all these blows thy head do hit,
> Thou with thy wife adult'ry shall commit. (*NA,* 295–96)

The last three lines of the oracle also contain variations, the most important of which is Sidney's shift from the *Old Arcadia*'s specific "All this on thee this fatal year shall hit" (*OA,* 5) to the *New Arcadia*'s indefinite "And ere that all these blows thy head do hit." I consider the change to be an attempt to excuse Pamela's elopement with Musidorus, which seems more justifiable in the *New Arcadia* because her marriage is postponed indefinitely, during which time Basilius's continued retirement threatens her life and the kingdom. Recall that when Fulke Greville published the incomplete *Arcadia* in 1590, English subjects were growing increasingly anxious over the succession, which Elizabeth refused to settle until 1603. This uncertain political climate helps to explain why readers welcomed the composite text, with its marital denouement, which Mary Sidney Herbert published as *The Countess of Pembroke's Arcadia* in 1593. An audience sympathetic to Pamela's elopement because it preserved the royal line would overlook its treasonable implications (which seem to have troubled Sidney himself).

22. Amphialus is, of course, as culpable as his mother in the imprisonment of Philoclea and Pamela. Although Cecropia kidnapped the princesses without his knowledge, Amphialus not only consents to her action but upholds it. When his mother ironically offers to release the prisoners, Amphialus conceals his complicity with vacillating rhetoric: "I would not for my life constrain presence—but rather would I die than consent to absence!" Cecropia's response to her son's speech—"Pretty, intricate follies!"—sums up my own evaluation of a character who wages civil war under the sign of chivalrous devotion to Philoclea (*NA,* 320).

23. For a survey of the most popular feminine stereotypes during the Renaissance, see the introduction to *Half Humankind: Contexts and Texts of the Controversy about Women in England, 1540–1640,* ed. Katherine Usher Henderson and Barbara F. McManus (Urbana: University of Illinois Press, 1985), 47–63.

24. Although Pamela uses the word "parents," the decision to retire is presented as her father's, not her mother's. In one of many guilty soliloquies, Gynecia interprets Basilius's decision as a destined test of her chastity rather than as an example of the king's foolish abuse of power: "For nothing else did my husband take this strange resolution to live so solitarily, for nothing else have the winds delivered this strange guest to my country, for nothing else have the destinies reserved my life to this time, but that only I, most wretched I, should become a plague to myself, and a shame to womankind" (*NA,* 120; cf. *NA* 17).

25. Claims to moral authority based on force are ironized throughout the *New Arcadia;* see Martin Raitiere, "Amphialus' Rebellion: Sidney's Use of History in the *New Arcadia," Journal of Medieval and Renaissance Studies* 12 (1982): 113–31, and Gordon Williams, "Humanist Responses to War: Sidney's Contribution," *Trivium* 16 (1981): 53–58. Williams suggests that the rape episode is an extension of Amphialus's decision to keep the princesses imprisoned: "In Spenserian style his [Amphialus's] delinquent self is reflected in the soldier-braggarts Anaxius and his brothers" (58). It is also worth noting that when Pyrocles acts for the princesses in the three episodes mentioned above, the violent actions of the "Amazon" are attributed to the same possessive and destructive impulses that motivate the men "she" attacks: in the tourney, "grief," "rage," and "jealousy" (*NA,* 100); at Ladon, "fury" and jealousy of "an unlooked-for rival" (*NA,* 196); and in the battle with Lycurgus, "wrath" at the sight of a token taken from Philoclea (*NA,* 462).

26. On the myth's variants during the period, see Turner-Wright, "Amazons," 451–53. Zelmane, frustrated by men who do not recognize matrilineal status, stoops to self-definition in masculine terms at two points in the narrative. The first occurs when Amphialus refuses to fight at Ladon and the Amazon promises him a rematch with her "near kinsman . . . Pyrocles, prince of Macedon" (*NA,* 197). The degree of their affinity becomes clear when, after Anaxius has also scorned Zelmane's challenge, the Amazon claims to be Pyrocles' half-sister, "begotten by his father of an Amazon lady" (*NA,* 454).

27. Traditionally, Amazons do not marry, a custom that Zelmane alters when she tries to trick the amorous Zoilus into giving her his weapons to "perform a vow which [she] made among [her] countrywomen, the famous Amazons, that [she] would never marry none, but such one as was able to withstand [her] in arms (*NA,* 46).

28. At the end of the *Old Arcadia* (when the obstacle to marriage is removed by Basilius's miraculous resurrection and change of heart), we learn that Musidorus, rather than Pamela, inherits the dukedom (*OA,* 417). It is worth noting that no woman who inherits a kingdom in the *New Arcadia* shows an inclination to remain unmarried; perhaps the instability of the succession during Elizabeth's reign accounts for the way that the fictional countries of her writing subjects, which were governed primarily by masculine desire, tended to feature female heirs who married early.

PART THREE

---

*Envisioning
the Hermaphrodite*

The Spiritual Eroticism of
Leone's Hermaphrodite

NAOMI YAVNEH

The discussion of man's creation in Leone Ebreo's *Dialoghi d'amore* (1535) constitutes a radical departure from traditional Renaissance Neoplatonism. Like Aristophanes in Plato's *Symposium*, Leone depicts the first human as a composite creature who is later divided into two beings, male and female. However, unlike other Renaissance commentators on Plato, particularly Ficino, Leone gives the fable a biblical origin. Moreover, whereas those other commentators follow Aristophanes in presenting this separation as punishment, Leone's version emphasizes that God divided man *before* the Fall, fashioning Eve out of Adam's side so that man and woman might enjoy each other and heighten their union through sexual intercourse.

This essay considers the *Dialoghi*'s treatment of both the biblical and Platonic creation narratives in the context of Leone's distinctive Neoplatonism. I hope to demonstrate that Leone's version of the creation story, and, indeed, the *Dialoghi* containing it, grants a different status to Plato than do other Neoplatonic texts of the period, particularly those of the so-called Platonic Academy of Florence. The founder of the Academy, Marsilio Ficino, virtually resurrected the study of Plato in late Quattrocento Italy; he devoted his life to the translation of Plato from Greek into Latin, as well as to textual commentary, and his massive *Theologia platonica* places Plato's writings in a position analogous to that of the Hebrew prophets in the Christian tradition. To Ficino and the other syncretists, both the philosopher Plato and the prophets point toward the truth of Christ's revelation. Charles Trinkaus has described Ficino's syncretism as an attempt "to create a new all-comprehensive mode of viewing man and God and the cosmos by combining the partial truths of the many preceding traditions into a new revelation or synthesis."[1] But as we shall see, Leone's syncretism is of a different kind; for Leone, a Portuguese Jew expelled from Spain in 1492, the Greek text serves a very different function from that of the Hebrew Bible.

Not much is known about Jehudah Abrabanel,[2] or Leone Ebreo, as he is known in Italy. He was born in Lisbon between 1460 and 1465, the son of the philosopher and biblical scholar Isaac. Isaac instructed his son in Talmud and Kabbalah, as well as Greek and Scholastic philosophy.[3] The *Dialoghi* was more than likely written sometime between 1501 and 1505, but was not published until 1535, in Rome.[4]

To those of us who have learned about Renaissance Neoplatonism principally by studying Ficino, perhaps the most striking feature of Leone's *Dialoghi* is its depiction of a dualistic cosmos governed by a system of universal hermaphrodism: Whereas eros is the *copula mundi* of Neoplatonic cosmology, Leone explicitly depicts that *copula* as heterosexual copulation. Not only is the universe divided between the masculine, active, and incorporeal and the feminine, passive, and corporeal, but these two sets of elements are depicted in terms of an anthropomorphic sexuality in which they continually seek union. The prime matter of the universe, Leone writes, is the feminine earth, *ricettaculo* (receptacle) of all the influences of her *maschio*, the heavens.

> Tutt'l corpo del cielo è il maschio che la copre e circonda con moto continuo. Ella, se ben è quieta, si muove pur un poco per il movimento del suo maschio. Ma l'umidita sua ch'è l'acqua, e il spirito suo ch'è l'aere, e il suo calor natural ch'è il fuoco, si muoveno attualmente per il moto celeste virile, secondo si muoveno tutte queste cose ne la femina al tempo del coito per il moto del maschio, se ben essa non si muove corporalmente, anzi sta quieta per ricevere il seme de la generazione del suo maschio.... Non vedi tu che non si continuaria una così somma diligenzia, così sottil provedimento, se non per un ferventissimo e finissimo amore che'l cielo, come proprio uomo generante, ha a la terra e agli altri elementi e ad essa prima materia in comune, come a propria donna de la qual sia innamorato over maritato con lei.... E la terra e materia ha amore al cielo come a dilettissimo marito, o amante, e benefattore.[5]

[All the heavens are the male, who covers and surrounds (the earth) with continual motion. Even though she is quiet, she nevertheless moves a little because of the movement of her male partner. But her moisture, which is water, and her spirit, which is the air, and her natural heat, which is fire, actually move through the motion of the virile heavens, just as all these elements move in the woman during coitus through the motion of the male, even if the woman does not actually move her body, but remains still to receive the seed of generation from her man.... Don't you see that such great diligence and such subtle and careful provisions would not continue if not through the most fervent and refined love that heaven—truly like a generating man—feels for the earth and the other elements and this prime matter in common, just as he would for a woman with whom he was in love or to whom he was married.... And the earth and prime matter loves Heaven just as she would a delightful husband, or lover, and benefactor.]

In his own sexuality, then, man is a microcosm, the *immagine,* or image, of the universe. God created man—Adam[6]—masculine and feminine and divided him into two beings, so that, as Leone states, "one might be a help before the other in coitus for procreation, the first intent of the Creator."[7]

Sexual intercourse is important not only for the generation of the species but also as a means of achieving spiritual union between opposites. The lover Filone tells Sofia,

> Non è il fine del perfetto amore: anzi il vincola più e collega con gli atti corporei amorosi; che tanto si desiderano quanto son segnali di tal reciproco amore in ciascuno de due amanti. Ancora perchè, essendo gli animi uniti in spirituale amore, i corpi desiderano la possibile unione, acciò che non resti alcuna diversità e l'unione sia in tutto perfetta; massime perchè, con la correspondenzia de l'unione corporale, il spirituale amore s'augmenta e si fa più perfetto. (50)

> [(Copulation) is not the end point of perfect love. . . . Rather, amorous corporeal acts serve to unite and bind lovers even more tightly, for the more each lover desires the other, the more this desire is a sign of reciprocal love in each of the two. Also, since the souls are united in spiritual love, the bodies desire all possible union, in order that no difference may remain between the two, and the union may be completely perfect. Most of all, when the corresponding physical union increases, so too does spiritual love, which becomes more perfect.]

Even man's highest goal, union with God, is described in terms of a sexual union: "Copulation," says Filone, "is the most correct and precise word which signifies beatitude."

In its double emphasis on spiritual union and physical procreation, the *Dialoghi* expresses a completely different view of sexuality from those of other Neoplatonic texts of the period, which celebrate an incorporeal, nonerotic, homosexual love. Works such as Ficino's *De amore* or Pico's *Commento* present spiritual desire in opposition to the inferior physical desire, which is at best a stopgap to be abandoned for a higher form of love and at worst a debasing and literally brutalizing passion. In such a view, procreation is denigrated as a mere physical function, a part of the corporeal realm that the true lover seeks to escape. But in the world of the *Dialoghi,* physical union is presented as a manifestation and reflection of a higher spiritual union; as such, it is not to be denied, but rather celebrated.

This celebration is not Leone's invention; Leone the Jew is writing more than an eroticized version of the *De amore.* In fact, the heterosexual emphasis of the *Dialoghi* reflects its roots in the Hebraic tradition. Whereas Pauline Christianity praises and encourages celibacy, Judaism stresses the need for a man to marry and procreate;[8] this ideological difference is clearly visible when we compare Leone to the Christian Ficino. God's first commandment is to "be fruitful and multiply" (Genesis 1:28) in order to perpetuate his image, for as we shall see, only when a man and a woman are together are they truly in the image of Adam, and thus of God. Rabbi Eleazar, quoted in the Talmudic tractate *Yebamoth*, says that "any man who has no wife is no proper man; for it is said, 'Male and female created he them and called their name Adam.'" The Kabbalistic *Zohar* expands the Talmudic discussion:

> R. Simeon said: "Profound mysteries are revealed in these two verses [Genesis 1:27–28]. The words 'male and female he created them' make known the high dignity of man, the mystic doctrine of his creation. . . . From [these words] we learn that every figure which does not comprise male and female elements is not a true and proper figure, and so we have laid down in the esoteric teaching of our Mishnah. Observe this. God does not place His abode in any place where male and female are not found together, nor are blessings found save in such a place, as it is written, AND HE BLESSED THEM AND CALLED THEIR NAME MAN ON THE DAY THAT THEY WERE CREATED: note that it says *them* and *their* name, and not *him* and *his* name. The male is not even called man till he is united with the female.[9]

It is this Judaic emphasis on the centrality of marriage and procreation that informs Leone's treatment of Plato and Genesis.

Leone's work is divided into three dialogues of varying lengths: "On Love and Desire," "On the Community of Love," and "On the Origins of Love." Each occurs between the lover Filone and his friendly but far from amorous beloved, Sofia. The third dialogue is by far the longest of the three, exploring the nature of love as well as all its accidents of origin—birth, source, location, and so forth. This dialogue's centerpiece is a complex discussion of the creation of man, an examination that juxtaposes the biblical creation story with the familiar fable of the hermaphrodite, or androgyne,[10] from the *Symposium*. I wish to explore this version of the creation story in the context of Leone's unique syncretism and the heterosexual cosmos just described.

In the third dialogue's discussion of love's origins, Filone repeats to Sofia the account of man's origins told by Aristophanes in Plato's *Symposium:* the first man is an androgyne, who, because he has rebelled against the gods, is divided into a masculine and a feminine portion. As in Plato, Filone's story demonstrates that love originates in the desire for reintegration, or wholeness:

> È dunque l'amor in ciascuno degli uomini, maschii e femmine, però che ognuno di loro è mezzo uomo e non uomo intero, onde ogni mezzo desia la reintegrazione sua con l'altro mezzo. Nacque adunque, secondo questa favola, l'amore umano de la divisione de l'uomo, e li suoi progenitori furono li dui sui mezzi, il maschio e la femmina, a fine di loro reintegrazione. (291)

[Thus is love in each human, masculine and feminine, because each of them is a half man, rather than an entire man. Accordingly, each half desires his reintegration with the other half, and thus, according to this fable, human love was born from the division of man, and love's parents were the two halves, masculine and feminine, who sought their own reintegration.]

Love, then, stems from a lack—the desire for union or copulation discussed in the first two dialogues—for each of us is created incomplete.

Filone's version of Aristophanes' fable, as well as his interpretation of its primary significance, remains remarkably close to the Platonic original, but with one very important difference: whereas the Greek text depicts double males and double females, as well as the androgyne, Filone asserts the existence only of a composite androgyne, and therefore only the androgyne revolts and is divided. His "correction" of the story makes it a much more clearly appropriate fable of origin for the heterosexual microcosm the *Dialoghi* depicts; Filone eliminates those elements that cannot be assimilated easily into his version of the cosmos. But the true significance of Filone's variation becomes apparent when Filone must explain its allegory. When Sofia asks the meaning of this "beautiful and ornate fable" (*favola bella e ornata*) the explanation is not a true explication but rather another story. Filone states that Plato's fable is really biblical in origin, translated "from an author more ancient than the Greeks: that is, from the sacred history of Moses of the creation of the first human parents, Adam and Eve."[11]

[Moses] Non l'ha già favoleggiata con questa particularità e chiarezza, ma ha posta la sustanzia sotto brevità, e Platone la prese da lui e l'ampliò e l'ornò secondo l'oratoria grecale, facendo in questo una mescolanza inordinata de le cose ebraiche. (291)

[Moses didn't recount the fable with this particularity and clarity, but rather gave the substance briefly. And Plato took the fable from him and amplified it and ornamented it according to the fashion of Greek oratory, making a disorderly mixture of the Hebrew parts.]

At first, the terms *particularità* and *chiarezza* appear to emphasize favorably the detail of the Platonic fable. Such a reading, however, is undermined when we learn that Plato's is a *mescolanza inordinata* —a disorderly mixture—of the crucial Hebrew elements from which it is composed. The relationship between the Hebrew and the Greek texts is thus paradoxical: in contrast to the Mosaic history, whose brevity conceals its complexity, the detail and seeming clarity of the Platonic fable obscure rather than reveal, for the allegory must be separated from those "particularities" that, in the words of Filone, are only ornaments to make the tale *"più bellà e verisimile."*

Such a characterization of the Platonic allegory eliminates for Leone an important dilemma faced by many other Renaissance commentators: namely, how to treat the homosexual emphasis of Plato's writings. Ficino, for example, while maintaining that the highest form of love occurs between men, nevertheless felt obliged to stress the nonphysical nature of such union and its distance not only from physical desire between men, which he terms base, but from heterosexual, procreative love: "That genital force of the soul has no power of cognition; it makes no discrimination between the sexes, so that those who associate with males have intercourse with them in order to satisfy the urge of their genital parts. . . . It is not pleasant to do. . . . Erection of the genital parts does not naturally bring about this ejaculation in vain, but for the purpose of procreation."[12] There is no need for such argumentative acrobatics in the *Dialoghi;* as we have seen, the eros of the *Dialoghi*'s heterosexual cosmology neither posits a distinction between earthly and heavenly love nor allows for homosexuality. Accordingly, Filone drops the homosexual elements from his telling of the story, for any details that do not coincide with his more Mosaic analysis can be included among the ornaments that, though pleasing to those Greeks, are irrelevant.

This radical revision of the Greek fable—the exclusion of homosexuality—points up the subordination of Plato's authority in the *Dialoghi*. Plato's *Symposium* is not presented as a divinely inspired text that is the source of an authoritative tradition *parallel* to the Hebraic tradition; rather, Plato is *absorbed* by the Hebraic tradition. For Leone, the sacred history dictated by God and transcribed by Moses is the source not only of the mysteries and fables of the Rabbis and Kabbalists but of Plato as well. The presence of the Hebraic tradition in the *Dialoghi* invokes not only a different view of sexuality but also a very different syncretic program from that found in the works of Pico or Ficino. Whereas Pico insists on a highly ordered universe expressed in the correspondences among widely divergent traditions, the discussion of Genesis in the *Dialoghi* emphasizes the centrality of the Hebrew Bible and the legitimacy of the Hebraic tradition as the matrix of wisdom and theology.[13]

Filone begins his discussion of the Bible by giving a synopsis of the Creation story. As he points out, the sacred story contains a contradiction, for whereas the first chapter of Genesis states, "And God created Adam in his own image; . . . male and female created he them" (Gen. 1:27), the second chapter narrates the formation of the woman out of the man's rib. Sofia suggests that such an apparent contradiction must point to an "occult mystery," and Filone confirms her suspicions: "In fact, Moses wants us to realize that he contradicts himself, and thus to search out the cause." Filone's explanation of the hidden mystery serves to emphasize the difference between Greek fable and sacred Hebrew text and to stress the superior didactic method of the latter, for whereas Plato's apparently ordered account is in fact a confusion, any seeming contradiction in the Bible is present specifically to draw the reader's attention to a puzzle that must be solved. As opposed to the beautiful and ornate fable of Plato, nothing in Genesis occurs by chance or merely for decor.

Nevertheless, the story of Genesis, as Filone explicates it, is in fact very close to the Platonic fable. The two creation stories are not contradictory but complementary. Filone, following Jewish Midrashic tradition, explains to Sofia that God originally created an Adam of two bodies, one masculine and one feminine, connected at the shoulders. God then divided Adam into two beings so that the female might help the male. Just as in the *Symposium,* desire is shown to be the result of the human's original nature; but here, that nature is explicitly described as heterosexual:

> Per essere divisi da un medesimo individuo, l'uomo e la donna si tornano e reintegrare nel matrimonio e coito in uno medesimo supposto carnale e individuale.

> [Because they are divided from the same individual, man and woman turn to each other and are rejoined through matrimony and coitus into one individual of flesh and blood.]

We must not forget that the Hebrew word *adam* is not initially a proper name in the Bible but rather the non-gender-specific term for humankind. The root is the same as that of *adamah,* the earth out of which Adam was formed.[14] According to Filone, Plato's source is not the Bible itself but "li commentari ebraici antichi in lingua caldea," the early rabbis, who wrote in Aramaic. Indeed, Filone's description is reminiscent of a passage in *Midrash Rabba,* especially when Filone emphasizes that the woman is formed not from Adam's *rib,* "costella," but his *side,* "lato":

> Rabbi Jeremiah ben Leazar said: When the Holy One, blessed be He, created Adam, He created him an hermaphrodite, for it is said, "Male and female created He them and called their name Adam." Rabbi Samuel ben Nahman said: When the Lord created Adam, He created him double-faced, then He split him and made him two backs, one back on this side and one back on the other side. To this it is objected: But it is written, "And He took one of his ribs . . . " (Gen.2:21). [Mi-zalothav means] one of his sides, replied he, as you read, "And for the second side [zela] of the tabernacle" (Ex.26:20).[15]

Filone's reference to the "commentari ebraici" is highly significant: by invoking commentators who were virtually unknown to his Christian audience, Leone places Plato at even further remove. It is not just the Hebrew Bible that is Plato's source—in itself an audacious claim—but the entire Rabbinic tradition that surrounds and explicates the Bible, a tradition obscure to the Gentile but central to the Jew.

But if Plato must be subordinated to Genesis, why is his fable the introduction to the discussion of the biblical narrative? We must remember that the *Dialoghi* was written for a Christian Italian audience, an educated audience far more familiar with the works of Plato than with any Hebrew texts. Ficino's Latin translations, as well as his elaborate commentaries, meant the Platonic corpus was widely read. But these same readers had very little contact with Hebrew texts other than through references made by the small number of Hebrew-reading Christian Neoplatonists. Such Christian readings of Jewish mysticism were informed by a radical typology; Pico della Mirandola states, in one of his nine hundred theses, "There is no greater proof of Christ's divinity than magic and the Kabbalah."[16] Placed in this historical context, Plato's role in the *Dialoghi* becomes more comprehensible: *within* the discourse of the third dialogue, Plato's text is secondary to the Bible, which is presented as the Greek's source. But the accepted stature of Plato *outside* the *Dialoghi* grants Leone Ebreo's discourse an authority it might otherwise have lacked in the Christian intellectual community.

Having explored the status of its sources, I would like to examine briefly the significance of the specifically hermaphroditic creation that Leone emphasizes. Like Moses' story of man's creation, Filone's explication of that narration contains a contradiction. He first tells Sofia that man and woman were divided for a good purpose: *la generazione,* the "first intent of the creator." Shortly afterward, however, Filone explains that man and woman were made with the possibility of reproduction but that "Man's true end is not to procreate, but to rejoice in divine contemplation and in God's paradise—having done this, they [Adam and Eve] would have remained immortal and would have had no need for procreation."[17] The problematic shift in tense (present indicative to past conditional) signals the source of contradiction, the enigma that the reader must strive to comprehend. The undivided Adam was created for contemplation only; procreation, although it is celebrated throughout the *Dialoghi,* is nevertheless a purely postlapsarian phenomenon, necessary only because of humanity's fallen state. For the first time in the entire work, Filone, the advocate of copulation, suggests the dangers of "carnal delectation, which appears good, but finally in principle and being is bad, because it diverts man from eternal life and makes him mortal."[18]

How are we to understand this seemingly abrupt shift in the *Dialoghi*'s interpretation of sexuality? Filone's contradictory statements require the reader to reexamine the complexity within Moses' brief description. According to Filone, *il primo intento* (the primary purpose) of the Hebrew "history" is to demonstrate that, although Adam was masculine and feminine, the two nevertheless were connected so as to promote spiritual, rather than physical, union: "The two parts were joined at the shoulders back to back: that is, their discourse was inclined neither toward coitus nor toward procreation, nor were they face to face, to accommodate such actions; rather, contrary to that inclination, their union was back to back—not that they were united corporeally but united in human essence and mental inclination—that is, both man and woman were united in divine contemplation."[19] The division, asserts Filone, was not for the purpose of procreation but rather so that man and woman might help each other. Indeed, Genesis 2 explains that God created woman as man's *ezer-k'negdo*, his helpmate. But, Filone explains, the division of male and female created the possibility of sin and thus became the source of sin. As originally created, the hermaphroditic Adam had neither the inclination nor the need to sin. Moreover, the female, weaker half could not be tempted so long as she was joined to the male, for the serpent lacked the "force and wisdom" (*forze e sagacità*) to deceive both of them. Once divided from the man, however, the woman was tempted by the serpent. The fallen pair covered their genitals, for carnal pleasure had diverted them from spiritual contemplation, "giving them the burden of procreation, the remedy of mortality."[20]

Filone's explication at this point appears to resemble the Augustinian interpretation of the Fall. In Saint Augustine's view, prelapsarian sexuality was without lust but would have served for procreation; book 14 of the *City of God* explains how, before the Fall, the male seed would have entered the womb through an act of will, without "lustful craving" and without loss of virginity.[21] Postlapsarian sexual arousal is thus both the sign and means of transmitting original sin. Adam was ashamed because his members "were being moved not by his own will" (*ad arbitrium voluntatis eius*) but by the instigation of libido, as if they had a will of their own (*arbitrium proprium*);[22] man's rebellion against God is epitomized in the "rebellion" of his flesh:

> After Adam and Eve disobeyed . . . they felt for the first time a movement of disobedience in their flesh, as punishment in kind for their own disobedience to God. . . . The soul, which had taken a perverse delight in its own liberty and disdained to serve God, was now deprived of its own original mastery over the body. . . . The sexual desire (*libido*) of our disobedient members arose in those first human beings as a result of the sin of disobedience . . . and because a shameless movement resisted the rule of their will, they covered their shameful members.[23]

For Filone, as for Augustine, eros is not the cause of the Fall; the sin is not sexuality per se but rather a lack of temperance, a "submersion" into sensuality. Filone tells Sofia that the serpent—"carnal delectation"—instructs the divided Adam in the *craft* of sexuality, granting him and his mate "much knowledge pertaining to lasciviousness and greed which before they lacked."[24] But Filone's interpretation of the Fall is in fact quite different from that of the Christian Augustine. The *Dialoghi* is concerned with the Creation story neither as an explanation of original sin nor as a condemnation of sexuality. We have seen that desire is the result of the human's original nature;[25] indeed, man is not complete, not the undivided Adam, unless joined to a woman.

The contradictory aspect of Filone's explication is more comprehensible when we recognize that the story of Adam's hermaphroditic creation is not only a historical allegory of humankind's original nature but also a moral allegory of how each of us must live. Filone tells Sofia,

> In uno specchio vedrai la vita di tutti gli uomini—il loro bene e male, conoscerai la vita che si debbe fuggire, e quella che si debbe sequire per venire a eterna beatitudine senza mai morire. (304)

> [In a mirror you will see the life of all men—their good and their bad. You will know the life which you must avoid, and the one which you must follow to reach eternal beatitude and immortality.]

Following the Talmudic tradition, Filone explains that every human's nature is hermaphroditic: "the first man, and every other man you see, is made, according to Scripture, in the image of God."[26] The masculine, says Filone, is the perfect, active intellect, whereas the feminine is the imperfect, passive body; in perfect union, the sensual feminine body is obedient to masculine reason and intellect. Nevertheless, the intellect needs the body for sustenance and procreation, so that, although there is a hierarchical relationship between the masculine and feminine aspects of the human, their relationship is likewise symbiotic, governed by the balance of opposites that informs the universe.

> Tutti gli amori e desideri umani nascono da la coalternata divisione de l'intelletto e corpo umano: pero che l'intelletto inclinato al corpo suo (come il maschio a la femmina) desia e ama le cose pertinenti a quello, e se sonon necessarie e moderate sono desideri e amori onesti per la loro moderazione et temperamento, se sono superflui sono lascivi e disoneste inclinazione e atti peccatori; ancora il corpo amando l'intelletto (come donna il marito maschio) si solleva in desiare le perfezioni di quello, sollecitando con li sentimenti, con gli occhi, con le orecchie e col senso, fantasia e memoria, d'acquistare il necessario per le rette cognizioni ed eterni abiti intellettuali, con che si felicità l'intelletto umano: e questi sono desideri e amori assolutamente onesti, e quanto più ardenti tanto più laudabili e perfetti. (307)

> [All human loves and desires are born from the division of the intellect and the body: so that the intellect inclined to its body (like the male to the female) desires and loves the things pertaining to (the body), and if they are necessary and moderate they are honest desires and loves because of their moderation and temperament, and if they are superfluous they are lascivious and dishon-

est inclinations and sinful acts; and the body loving the intellect (like a woman her husband) desires his perfection, seeking with sentiments, with her eyes, her ears and her sense, her fantasy and memory, to acquire what is necessary for proper cognition and eternal intellectual garments, in which the intellect rejoices: and these are absolutely honest desires and loves, and the more ardent they are, the more they are praiseworthy and perfect.]

Filone's description of human nature calls to mind the cosmological discussion from dialogue 2 cited earlier. That discussion emphasizes an eros of generative union that is both physical and spiritual. We are told that "the man who, with reason, preserves himself in worthy and excellent love without enjoying or tasting it, is like a tree which is always green, with greatly abundant branches, but with no fruit—a tree which truly can be called sterile." Yet the hermaphrodite Adam is a sterile being who, like the planets to which Filone compares him, would have no reason for generation. Although Adam was originally created for contemplation, God's decision to divide the woman from the man was a decision to create a dynamic universe in which the movement of intercourse is the remedy for disunion as well as mortality; the sexual tension created by the Fall is the generating force of the universe, just as the same erotic tension of desire literally informs the fictive *Dialoghi* between the wise Filone and the Sofia whom he loves in vain.

Leone's biblical account of the Fall denies the typology that transforms Mary into a second Eve whose virgin birth provides restitution for her forebearer's sin. But the lack of a Christian ontology is not the only distinctive feature of Leone's Jewish Neoplatonism; rather, the *Dialoghi d'amore* seeks to express the dignity of man in all his parts.[27] Leone's is not just a celebration of the human spirit but of the entire human, male and female, whose creative capacity originates in the procreative powers granted by God to His own image.

NOTES

Earlier versions of this paper were presented at the 1989 Conference of the Renaissance Society of America, held at Harvard University, March 30–April 1, and at the 1988 Southwest Regional Renaissance Conference at the Huntington Library in Pasadena, on April 15–16. I wish to thank Joshua Kosman, Patrick Cook, and the members of Paul Alpers's dissertation group at the University of California at Berkeley for their careful readings and thoughtful comments on those versions.

1. Charles Trinkaus, *In Our Image and Likeness* (Chicago: University of Chicago Press, 1970), 504. See also Ernst Cassirer, *The Individual and the Cosmos in Renaissance Philosophy* (Philadelphia: University of Pennsylvania Press, 1963); Ronald Levao, *Renaissance Minds and Their Fictions* (Berkeley: University of California Press, 1985),

106–11; and Edgar Wind, *Pagan Mysteries in the Renaissance* (New York: W. W. Norton and Company, 1968).

2. The last name is variously spelled Abravanel and Abarbanel; the *Encyclopedia Judaica* (Jerusalem: Keter Publishing House, 1972) s. v. "Abrabanel," declares Abrabanel to be the proper form.

3. For biographical information, see the introduction to the edition of the *Dialoghi* edited by Santino Carmella (Bari:haterza, 1929). See also Riccardo Scrivano, "Platonic and Cabalistic Elements in the Hebrew Culture of Renaissance Italy: Leone Ebreo and his *Dialoghi d'amore*," in *Ficino and Renaissance Neoplatonism*, ed. Olga Zorzi Pugliese and Konrad Eisenbichler (Ottawa: Dovehouse Editions Canada, 1986), and the articles on Jehudah, Isaac, and the Abrabanel family in the *Encyclopedia Judaica*.

4. There has been some debate as to whether the *Dialoghi* was written originally in Italian or Hebrew, and thus as to the text's original intended audience. The work was first published in Italian, and we can assume at any rate that the *Dialoghi*, at least the published version, was addressed to a Gentile readership. A far more interesting question is posed by Riccardo Scrivano: "Do the *Dialoghi* constitute the attempt made by a Jewish intellectual, suffering deep trauma for not having achieved integration into Western society, to find an acceptable mode of being, without renouncing the culture of his forefathers, by showing the common origin of the doctrines of both worlds ... ? Or ... is the treatise the consistent effort made by a believer and intellectual, exceptionally gifted beyond learning, education, and mind, to show that, beyond the existing divisions, everything stems from a single true and authentic dimension, that is Hebraism?" ("Platonic Elements," 126). As this essay attests, my own views tend toward the latter interpretation.

5. Leone Ebreo, *Dialoghi d'amore,* ed. Santino Carmella (Bari: haterza, 1929), 80–83. Hereafter, page numbers will be cited in the text, and all references are to this edition. All translations are mine.

6. The Hebrew word *adam* is the non-gender-specific term for humans.

7. " ... perchè potessero aiutarsi l'uno nel fronte de l'altro nel coito per la generazione, primo intento del creatore" (296). As interlocutors, Sofia and Filone represent two halves of an androgyne, or hermaphrodite, just as their names together form "philosophy."

8. I use the term "man" advisedly. As Maryanne Cline Horowitz discusses in her article, "The Image of God in Man—Is Woman Included?" *Harvard Theological Review* 72 (1979): 175–206, the Talmudic rabbis, while insisting that marriage was the proper state for all humans, debated whether woman as well as man was commanded to procreate. Horowitz cites a Mishnah in Tractate *Yebamoth* (65a–b): "A man is commanded concerning the duty of propagation, but not a woman" (188).

9. *The Zohar,* trans. Harry Sperling and Maurice Simon (London: Soncino Press, 1984), 55b.

10. Throughout this essay, the terms "hermaphrodite" and "androgyne" are used interchangeably, although I favor the former. Carla Freccero has stressed the "distinction between the terms androgyne and hermaphrodite, the former being a spiritualized union of male and female aspects, the latter connoting a monstrous

hybrid, characterized not only by a merging of the two sexes, but by the deformation of each required to effect the union" ("The Other and the Same," in *Rewriting the Renaissance* [Chicago: University of Chicago Press, 1986], 149). To support this distinction, Freccero discusses the story of Hermaphroditus found in Ovid's *Metamorphoses*. But as we shall see, in Filone's treatment of Genesis, the hermaphrodite is perhaps the most perfect form, for the hermaphroditic Adam alone was truly in God's image. For discussions of the hermaphrodite, see Mircea Eliade, *The Two and the One* (New York: Sheed and Ward, 1965); and Marie Delcourt, *Hermaphrodite: Mythes et rites de la bisexualité dans l'antiquité classique* (Paris: P.G.F., 1958).

11. "... la favola è tradutta da autore più anitco de li greci, cioè da la sacra istoria di Moise de la creazione de li primi parenti umani Adam ed Eva" (291).

12. Marsilio Ficino, *De amore* (Commentary on Plato's *Symposium*), ed. and trans. Sears Reynolds Jayne (Dallas: Spring Publications, 1985), sixth speech. It is interesting to note that Ficino's allegorical treatment of Aristophanes' speech completely obliterates the sexual aspects of the fable. In Ficino's reading, the Platonic androgyne represents the souls of men, which, when whole, were "equipped with two lights, one natural, one supernatural. 'They aspire to equal God'; they reverted to the natural light alone. Hereupon, they were divided, and lost their supernatural light, were reduced to natural light alone, and fell immediately into bodies."

13. Leone is not the only Renaissance philosopher to present the Hebraic tradition as the source of Plato's knowledge. See, for example, the discussion in D. P. Walker, *The Ancient Theology: Studies in Christian Platonism from the Fifteenth Century to the Eighteenth Century* (Ithaca: Cornell University Press, 1972); and Frances Yates, *Giordano Bruno and the Hermetic Tradition* (Chicago: University of Chicago Press, 1964). But whereas other Renaissance Neoplatonists see the Old Testament in turn as a prophetic source of Christianity, for Leone, the Hebraic tradition is the central tradition; the Old Testament is *the* Bible, *the* sacred text.

14. Although the word *adam* is masculine in gender, *adamah* is a feminine noun.

15. *Bereshit Rabbah,* trans. H. Freedman and Maurice Simon (London: Soncino Press, 1961), 8:1. I am thankful to Rabbi Pinchas Giller for first drawing my attention to this passage. The verse cited by Rabbi Jeremiah is used also by the rabbis in the Talmud to support the belief that only man and woman together—that is, married—are in the image of God.

16. "Nulla est scientia que nos magis certificet de divinitate Christus quam magia et cabala."

17. "... il proprio fine de l'uomo non è il generare, ma felicitarsi ne la contemplazione divina e nel paradiso di Dio, in che facendo restavano immortali e non bisognavano di generazione" (298).

18. "... la dilettazione carnale, che è buona in apparenzia nel principio e ne l'esistenzia in fine è gattiva, che diverte l'uomo da la vita eterna e lo fa mortale" (298).

19. "Il primo intento de l'istoria ebraica è mostrare che ... se bene [l'uomo] era maschio e femmina ... niente di manco questi due supposti e parti di uomo in quello stato beato erano colligati in le spalle per contra viso: cioè che la conferenzia

loro non era inclinato a coito nè a generazione, nè il viso de l'uno si drizzava in fronte a l'altro viso, come suole per tale effetto; anzi, come alienati da tale inclinazione, dice l'unione loro essere per contra viso, non che fussero uniti corporalmente ma uniti in essenzia umana e inclinazine mentale, cioè tutti due a la beata contemplazione divina" (297).

20. " . . . dandogli cura de la generazione e procreazione de' figli, remedio de la sua mortalità (298).

21. "The male seed could have been dispatched into the womb of the fertile wife with no loss of female virginity (*integritate*), just as the menstrual flux can now be produced from the womb of a virgin with no loss of virginity. For the seed could be injected through the same passage by which the flux is ejected. Now just as the female viscera might have been opened for parturition by a natural impulse when the time was ripe, instead of by the groans of travail, so the two sexes might have been united for impregnation and conception by an act of will, instead of by a lustful craving." St. Augustine, *The City of God,* 14.26, cited in James Turner, *One Flesh: Paradisal Marriage and Sexual Relations in the Age of Milton* (Oxford: Clarendon Press, 1987), 46.

22. Augustine, *De gratia et peccato originale,* cited in Turner, *One Flesh,* 44.

23. Augustine, *De civitate dei* 13.13, 13.24, cited in Elaine Pagels, *Adam, Eve, and the Serpent* (New York: Random House, 1988), 110–11.

24. " . . . conosceranno molte cose . . . di simil natura, che innanzi non conoscevano, cioè molte astuzie e cognizioni pertinenti a la lascivia o avarizia, di che innanzi erano privati" (301).

25. "Because they are divided from the same individual, man and woman turn to each other and are rejoined through matrimony and coitus into one individual . . . " (*Dialoghi,* 300).

26. "Il primo uomo, e ogni altro uomo di quanti ne vedi, è fatto, come dice la Scrittura, a immagine e similitudine di Dio, maschio e femmina" (209).

27. I use the term "man" advisedly. Although Leone emphasizes both the physical and spiritual aspects of the human and grants primacy to heterosexual love, the *Dialoghi* nevertheless insists that the male holds the superior hierarchical position.

The Bisexual Portrait of Francis I: Fontainebleau, Castiglione, and the Tone of Courtly Mythology

RAYMOND B. WADDINGTON

One of the more bizarre sixteenth-century works of art, tantalizing out of all proportion to its aesthetic value, is a small painting, executed on parchment pasted to wood, now cautiously attributed to Niccolò Bellin da Modena. Bellin da Modena had been *valet de la garde-robe* to Francis I from 1516 until 1522. After a ten-year absence, he reappeared in Francis's service as an assistant to Primaticcio, working on the Chambre du Roi at Fontaine-bleau, thereafter becoming qualified as "sculptor and mask-maker." Later charged with embezzlement, in 1537 he fled to England, where he remained in the service of successive monarchs until his death in 1569.[1] Fittingly, his painting takes as its subject his first master, Francis I, whose godlike quali-ties it celebrates in a composite, bisexual portrait (fig. 1).

The viewer's eye is arrested first by the extraordinary equipage and dress in which the king is represented. Francis wears an outsized, plumed helmet with the beaver raised. His armored right arm holds upright a short sword; his bare left arm is at his side, holding above a caduceus and below an unstrung bow. Slung across his back is a partially visible quiver of arrows, and a hunting horn is fastened at his right side. On his feet Francis has sandals; wings are attached to his heels. His ornamental breastplate displays the serpent-haired visage of Medusa; the armor of his right arm terminates in a lion-headed shoulderplate. He wears a knee-length red tunic hemmed with a golden fringe, beneath which a pale green undergarment extends. The sling of the quiver and the belt that bunches the tunic at his haunches are in a harsh green. The caduceus, visor, sword hilt, sandal straps, and the like are in gold. In explanation of this strange ensemble of costume and attributes, verses are inscribed on the cartouche, which serves as a pedestal for the king's figure:

> FRancoys en guerre est vn Mars furieux
> En paix Minerue et diane a la chasse

F Rancoys en guerre eſt vn Mars furieux
En paix Minerue & diane a la chaſſe
A bien parler Mercure copieux
A bien aymer vray Amour plein de grace
O france heureuſe honore donc la face
De ton grand Roy qui ſurpaſſe Nature
Car l'honorant tu ſers en meſme place
Minerue, Mars, Diane, Amour, Mercure

1. Attributed to Niccolò Bellin da Modena, *Francis I,* engraving by P. Chenu
(Bibliothèque Nationale, Paris).

A bien parler Mercure copieux
A bien aymer vray Amour plein de grace
O france heureuse honore donc la face
De ton grand Roy qui surpasse Nature
Car l'honorant tu sers en mesme place
Minerve, Mars, Diane, Armour, Mercure

[François in war is a furious Mars,
In peace Minerva and Diana of the hunt,
A well-spoken, copious Mercury,
A much-loving, true Amor full of grace.
O fortunate France, honor this face
Of your great king who surpasses Nature,
For there you will have honored in the same place
Minerva, Mars, Diana, Amor, Mercury.]

Even with the guidance of this doggerel, the figure of Francis appears a grotesque one and it is easy to empathize with Françoise Bardon's reaction: "Il y a quelque chose de déconcertant et presque de monstrueux dans la conception de cette figure virile, en jupe de femme, où le bras nu de Vénus s'oppose au bras de Mars et où le déhanchement est tellement accusé." [There is something disconcerting and almost monstrous in the design of this manly figure, dressed in a woman's skirt, where the bare arms of Venus contrast with the arms of Mars and where the leaning posture is so pronounced.][2] Oddly, however, Bardon proceeds to undermine this response by pointing to the appearance of composite gods and mythological personages in emblem books and in the ceremonies of royal *entrées* and *pompes funèbres*.[3] Her rationale is shared by leading art historians. André Chastel, commenting on the mode of symbolic portraiture, remarks, "They encouraged an idealizing conception of the world: the subject being disguised as a classical God or Goddess, or even, in a curious, but perfectly serious, mannerist portrait of Francis I, as a composite god."[4] Edgar Wind elaborates:

> Among French humanists of the sixteenth century *l'androgyne de Platon* became so acceptable an image for the universal man that a painter could apply it without impropriety to an allegorical portrait of Francis I. The shock of seeing the bearded warrior display the anatomy of a *virago* is lessened by the emblematic style of the painting which reduces the portrait to a hieroglyphic design, a mystical cipher of divine perfection.... In their extravagance these courtly compliments revert to a primitive way of picturing the numinous; they conceive of the supernatural as a composite.[5]

The difficulty with this line of interpretation is that the style of Bellin da Modena's painting is not emblematic, making it impossible to see the portrait as simply "idealizing" and "perfectly serious."

The objection is quickly substantiated by comparing some genuinely emblematic composite figures. Bardon cites the title page woodcut from Simeoni's *Devises ou emblèmes héroïques et morales* (Lyon, 1561); but this figure of Mars with the caduceus of Mercury is not composite. No more pertinent is her reference to Niccolò Stopio's "Hermathena," for the image of Hermes and Athena embracing also is not composite.[6] We do not lack examples of genuine composite figures—for instance, the emblem book combinations of soldier and scholar, active and contemplative lives, pen and sword. But, as in the Mars-Mercury emblem from Sir Henry Goodyere's *Mirrovr of Majestie* (London, 1618), these are abstract constructs, figures split in half and stuck to others as if by Super Glue.[7] Adriano Fiorentino's medal of Ferdinand II of Aragon has a reverse of a bisexual, composite head—a bearded and aged male to the left and a younger female to the right (fig. 2). This Janiform construct evokes the Prudence tradition in its balance of qualities; its abstract, symbolic projection is heightened by the blank background and the lack of contact between the head and the upright sword suspended on the right.[8] The two faces are not sex- and age-adapted versions of the same head but merely two different halves grafted together, resulting in neither human monstrosity nor idealization but in direct conceptualization.

Even more tellingly, we can gauge Bellin da Modena's distance from an emblematic style by looking at a medal of Henri II (fig. 3), dated 1552, that adapts the portrait of Francis I to a celebration of his son's military successes against the Hapsburg Empire.[9] The intention here is unmistakably idealizing and laudatory; hovering figures of Victory and Peace hold a laurel crown over Henri's head, and the surrounding legend proclaims, "ET PACE ET BELLO ARMA MOVET." The rather cluttered reverse presents Fame, driving a quadriga and holding her trumpet, to which is attached a flag with the fleur-de-lis; Victory and Plenty, with her cornucopia, are seated to her right. The legend specifies that this medal honors military successes in Italy, Germany, and France.

The artist's alterations of Bellin da Modena's Francis I figure define the peculiar character of the original in a fascinating way. Some of these are simplifications of costume and attributes. The cumbersome, plumed helmet is omitted, as are the winged sandals of Mercury. The contrasting armored right arm and bare left arm (now balanced by a bare right leg) remain; Cupid's quiver of arrows is gone, although his bow, now strung for action, stays. Diana's hunting horn, Mercury's caduceus, Minerva's Medusan breastplate, the leonine shoulder ornament, and the sword of Mars, now enlarged to a proper battle sword, are all retained; the drapery of the tunic is simplified and tidied. But it is the treatment of the body itself that especially alerts us to the quality of Bellin da Modena's portrait and to the

2. Adriano Fiorentino, medal of Ferdinand II of Aragon (National Gallery of Art, Washington, D.C.).

3. Medal of Henri II (British Museum, London).

deficiency of an analysis that concentrates exclusively on the symbolic attributes. Such an analysis would be valid for the Henri II medal, which presents the king directly as an icon, but the Francis I portrait is something else entirely.

Simply put, Bellin da Modena has given Francis the head of a man and the body of a woman—a woman, moreover, who conforms fully to contemporary taste in feminine beauty. To be exact, the body and costume shade elements of High Renaissance figuration into traits distinctly identifiable from the current Mannerist style. The conception of the torso is in the older manner, as Anne Hollander has described it: "[a] neat, tightly clad upper body,with the sweeping outward curve of the belly below, creating the look of considerable distance between the raised waistline and the lowered pelvis, where the hip joint bends when the figure is seated. The female torso is thus elongated through the middle."[10] Although the breastplate, straps, and armor frustrate close inspection, the breasts are fashionably minimal. The bare arm is feminine, slender, and unmuscled; but, unlike the emblematic, composite figures, the other arm can be no more substantial beneath the armor. To compensate for the elongated torso, the legs have been lengthened in typical Mannerist fashion. Mannerist too are the rather elegantly small hands and feet, with precisely individuated fingers and toes. The head also would appear small for the body were it not for the oversized Minervan helmet. But the magnet for the viewer's eyes is the exaggeratedly protuberant stomach. Hollander remarks, "In the erotic imagination of Europe, it was apparently impossible until the late seventeenth century for a woman to have too big a belly."[11] Indeed, she finds the enlarged belly becomes so conventional a sign of beauty that other indicators of gesture and clothing must be contrived to signify pregnancy. Bellin da Modena gives his monarch a body that displays beauty and erotic appeal, not fertility. In a touch characteristic of the Fontainebleau school, the tunic is stretched over the belly to reveal the navel. Finally, the entire body is positioned in an anatomical impossibility that would have gladdened Bronzino's heart. The shoulders are turned to the right, the belly and pelvis twist improbably from right back to center, a slightly upraised right knee gives the legs a thrust off center, and the whole is governed by the *linea serpentinata* of which the Fontainebleau artists were so fond.[12] Surmounting all this, we have a recognizably naturalistic head of Francis I, ruefully looking out at us: middle-aged, sparsely bearded, the eyes wary and the expression unpleased, uncomfortable, a bit sheepish, and unheroic.

By contrast, the Henri II medalist not only has simplified the accoutrements and signaled unambiguously his intentions through the crowning genii, he also has regularized and classicized bodily proportions and posture. Gone are the *linea serpentinata* distortions and contortions. Rather than looking out at the beholder, Henri looks to the right, presenting a profile that, Jones notes, is a standard portrait type from his coinage. His torso is squarely forward, the elongation and the swelling belly are eliminated, and the disproportions of small head and long legs are corrected. The visible musculature of the bared arm and calf is more developed and pronouncedly masculine. Similarly, the modifications of costume—for example, the king's exposed knees and the diminished ornamentation—make it possible to accept this figure as a warrior clad *all'antica,* poised for action with his right foot raised to step forward, his weapons held more resolutely and at the ready than his predecessor's. Far from appearing with a woman's body and dress, this king is a battle-ready commander with a man's body in a neutral costume, already partially stripped to fight. This icon of military leadership presents a thoroughly masculine figure with two almost incidental and hardly recognizable attributes of feminine divinities, breastplate and hunting horn. The artist has performed a successful sex-change operation on Bellin da Modena's monstrously bisexual Francis I.

What kind of thing is that to say about a king? To even approach grasping the tone of Niccolò Bellin da Modena's painting, it is necessary to consider the character and personal mythology of Francis I, as well as the translation of his personality and taste into the subjects, themes, and style of the art at Fontainebleau. Francis's multifaceted activities, talents, and interests—as courageous soldier, athlete, enthusiastic hunter, Machiavellian diplomat, masker, poet, and serious patron of the arts—made him a virtual embodiment of the ideal Renaissance prince, but his image in popular legend as a relentless and licentious seducer overshadows his more substantial achievements, remaining sufficiently potent after three centuries to inspire Hugo's play *Le Roi s'amuse* and, from it, the amoral duke of Verdi's *Rigoletto.*

In a dispassionate sifting of the evidence regarding the character and reputation of Francis, his most recent biographer comments that many discreditable stories are the fabrication of Bourbon authors writing well after Francis's lifetime, just as the more modern negative assessments of his person and reign can be associated with the republican biases of nineteenth-century historians.[13] Nonetheless, a considerable volume of pejorative evidence and testimony from Francis's time remains. By the time of his accession in 1515, Francis was carrying on an affair with the wife of a prominent citizen. Mary Tudor complained that the king had been "importunate with her in divers matters not to her honour."[14] In his early twenties, Francis was given to leading his favorites on riotous, masked expeditions to the bordellos of Paris. An English visitor records that they "roade daily disguysed through Parys, throwyng Egges, stones and other foolishe trifles at the people, which light demeanoure of a kyng was muche discommended and gested at."[15] The king's licentiousness became one of the recurrent motifs of his reign. In 1517 Antonio De Beatis wrote in his journal, "The king . . . is a great womaniser and readily breaks into other's gardens and drinks at many sources."[16] Presumably, this indiscriminate thirst brought its own punishment; by 1524 Francis was rumored to be sick "of his own French disease," syphilis, and it seems likely that he died from the consequences of a venereal infection.[17] His appetite, however, did not decline. Four years before his death, a courtier wrote, "our master's conduct is as you have always described it to me: the further he goes, the more he gets caught up with women, and he is quite shameless about it."[18] Pope Paul III, on hearing the news of Francis's death in 1547, reportedly compared the king's morals to those of Sardanapalus.

The nineteenth-century historian Jules Michelet epitomized Francis's education in two nouns, *"les femmes, la guerre"* (women, war), which he aphoristically conjoined: *"la guerre pour plaire aux femmes"* (war to please women).[19] Like many drastic oversimplifications, this one is not without its bedrock of truth. Aside from his boundless erotic attraction to the species in general, Francis's reign was marked to a considerable extent by his domination by a few women in particular. In the first ten to fifteen years, three were influential: Queen Claude, of whom he seemed genuinely fond, who gave him seven children and died in 1524; his sister, Marguerite de Navarre, author of the *Heptameron,* who, although wasted in an unhappy marriage, retained her interest in the court and in foreign affairs; and undoubtedly the most considerable, his mother, Louise of Savoy, who served as regent on Francis's two Italian military incursions and wielded power in various spheres. The English ambassador advised Cardinal Wolsey that "he [Francis] is so obeissant to her that he will refuse nothing that she requireth him to do."[20] During the unexpectedly extended second regency that resulted from Francis's year-long captivity after his defeat at Pavia (February 1525), Louise moved resolutely to defend the kingdom against invasion, faced down opposition to a woman regent, dealt dexterously with the Parlement, and successfully negotiated the king's ransom. Later, she was a principal—with Margaret of Savoy, her sister-in-law—in negotiating the treaty of Cambrai, the so-called Peace of the Ladies, which bought Francis four years respite in his clashes with Charles V.[21]

When Louise died in 1531, another female star already was ascending on Francis's horizon. After his release from captivity in March 1526, he met Anne d'Heilly, who was then an eighteen-year-old maid-of-honor to Louise. Anne soon eclipsed Françoise de Foix, comtesse de Chateaubriant, his first official mistress. Within a year, as was reported to Henry VIII, she had established her preeminence in the cluster of court ladies surrounding

Francis: " . . . a great number of ladies and gentlewomen, used to be in his company be sent for, and there he passes his time until ten or eleven o'clock, among whom above others . . . he favours a maiden of Madame de Vendome, called Hely whose beauty, after my mind, is not highly to be praised."[22] Whether or not she appealed to English taste in beauty, Anne d'Heilly proved to be a distance runner. By 1531 she was observed lending solace to Francis, who—through the terms of the recent treaty—was now the reluctant benedict of Eleanor, the emperor's sister, with whom his displeasure was public knowledge:

> For the first, being both in one house they lie not together once in four nights; another he speaks very seldom unto her openly; another, he is never out of my lady's chamber, and all for Hely's sake, his old lover . . . and the same day [the Queen] should make her entry into Paris, he, having knowledge where Hely and divers other ladies and gentlewomen stood . . . the French king took Hely and set her before him in an open window and there stood devising with her two long hours in the sight and face of all the people, which was not a little marvelled at of the beholders.[23]

After the death of Louise of Savoy, Anne became governess of the king's daughters. In 1534 Francis married her to Jean de Brosse, seigneur de Penthièvre, gifting the nuptial pair with the county of Etampes, which he elevated later to a dukedom. Continuing to live at court despite her marriage, Anne, now the duchesse d'Etampes, was notorious for the tyrannical meddling in politics and patronage that Cellini's *Life* portrays so vividly and that made her a power to be reckoned with until, after the king's death in 1547, she was dispossessed, sued, briefly imprisoned, and banished to a country estate.[24] Such were the women in Francis's life.

That a prince's taste in art might reflect his personality and recreational interests should surprise no one. The more intriguing issues concerning Francis, as Chastel has suggested, lie in the surprising outlet for this taste and the prodigality with which it was indulged: "We are immediately confronted with the most inexplicably strange and disturbing element of the Fontainebleau phenomenon: the unexpected decision in 1528 to embellish an undistinguished manor-house on the edge of the Forest of Bievre—for which a reckless and excitable king, returning from a particularly humiliating captivity, showed a strong predilection. It sprang thus from the need for prestige and from caprice."[25] Francis's commitment to the arts was a long-standing one; early in his reign he brought Leonardo and Andrea del Sarto to France and amassed a significant collection, featuring Florentine and Roman artists.[26] The decision to re-create Fontainebleau as a suitable principal residence, an image of his own magnificence, gave him the first chance—opportunely advanced by the artistic diaspora after the sack of Rome—not merely to collect but to direct, placing the stamp of his own personality on a large-scale artistic program.[27] Moreover, as the conception of Fontainebleau evolved, the systematic dissemination of prints permitted artistic patronage to be apprehended and admired, for the first time, from whatever distance.[28]

Definitions of the school of Fontainebleau understandably tend to fuse subject and style. The viewer's attention divides almost evenly between the narrative subjects and the prominent ornamentation: hybrids of paint and stucco, grotesque and comically exaggerated frames, cartouches, pedestals, and strapwork; riotously energetic combinations of the animate, the natural, and the geometric; satyrs, nymphs, and putti in writhing juxtaposition to swags of fruit and ostentatious scrolls. The typical subject is the female nude in a mythological scene or episode, amorous in nature: the loves of Jupiter, Diana and her attendants, Venus bathing. An art of surfaces, deliberately eschewing psychological or religious motivation, heightens and intensifies its own preoccupation with the allure of feminine beauty: "The women of Fontainebleau seem made of enamel. Whether reclining, sitting or standing, their bodies are usually turned. These bodies are elongated in the legs, in the body, and in the neck, and their fingers and toes are well separated. An identifying characteristic of the school is the elaborate coiffures of the women."[29] Chastel insists that, although this art is divorced from the moralist tradition, the tone of caprice and the weight of mythological symbolism remove it from licentiousness, "creating an almost joyful relationship between sensuality and sublimation."[30] Henri Zerner adds, "Moreover, it is not a matter only of a visual vocabulary, a world of forms. It is tied up with a repertory of themes—one might call it an iconographic style—which stresses the courtly, erotic and ambiguously sensual character, restless without anguish, of this sophisticated art."[31]

The first, and possibly decisive, recruitment to the troop of artists to work on Fontainebleau was Rosso Fiorentino. The circumstances are worth recounting. Commencing in 1529, for several years Pietro Aretino served Francis as an artistic talent scout, eventually being rewarded with the famous chain of gold tongues familiar from various portraits of Aretino. Perhaps not coincidentally, Aretino already had achieved notoriety for the pornographic sonnets he wrote to complement the Giulio Romano–Marcantonio Raimondi engravings, *I modi*. Following the sack of Rome, Rosso's peripatetic course eventually brought him to Venice, where he enjoyed Aretino's hospitality and executed a drawing of *Mars and Venus* for his host in the spring or summer of 1530. It has been conjectured that the drawing was commissioned, or at least suggested, by Aretino to celebrate the marriage of Francis I to Eleanor of Portugal, sister of Charles V, in fulfillment of the treaty of Cambrai.[32] The marriage was solemnized on 7 July; presumably, the drawing was sent to Francis and met with his approval, because by October Rosso is known to have been in France and in the king's service. Indeed, he made such a good impression on the king that Francis appointed him his First Painter. The association seems to have been a successful one; Vasari reports that, at the news of Rosso's death in 1540, Francis lamented that "it caused him indescribable regret, since it was his opinion that in losing Rosso he had been deprived of the most excellent artist of his time."[33]

The drawing depicts a youthful, beardless Mars standing beside the bed of Venus while she sits on its edge, one leg on the bed and the other on the floor (fig. 4). The two prospective lovers are caught being undressed by their attendants. On the right, Cupid strips Mars's last remaining garment from his shoulders; to the extreme left, one of the Graces undoes Venus's girdle; in the center and on the far right, her sisters hold back the drapery of the bed and the entry. Above, putti tumble and frolic, tossing flowers and shooting arrows; below, more putti play with Mars's discarded identifying armor. (Without it, he easily might be taken for Adonis.) Venus stretches her right arm in a come-hither gesture, but Mars, shrugging out of his tunic, appears to shrink from her. His petulant, open-mouthed grimace confirms the body language. Noting that the flowers thrown by the putti are the lilies of France and the roses of Venus, Jean Adhémar has concluded that "Mars relinquishing his arms to devote himself to Venus can be taken, therefore, as an allegory of Francis I."[34] His argument has been widely accepted. Eugene A. Carroll, for instance, assents, "In this highly sophisticated drawing Rosso, through his wit and style, must subtly have intended to encourage the monarch to recognize that his political defeat could have its artistic rewards."[35]

The argument is an attractive one. The hero of Marignano had been reduced to the ignominious loser of Pavia, a captive who had to be ransomed by his mother. Even more humiliatingly, his release was effected only by the substitution of his two sons as hostages; their return, in exchange for the necessary ransom, was obtained with the quite literal accompaniment of his enemy's sister, the new queen, Eleanor. Given Francis's reputation as a man devoted to amorous adventure he might well feel himself, after the fatal Cleopatra of Pavia, in a position like that of Shakespeare's Mark Antony, ready to undertake "no wars without doors." All of this was public knowledge, easy enough for Aretino to shape as a subtext to Rosso's invention. Yet the risk to Rosso and Aretino seems considerable. Why should Francis be expected to welcome and reward a projection of himself that, however witty and subtle, calls attention to the embarrassment of his defeat, submission, and enforced marriage?

4. Rosso Fiorentino, *Mars and Venus* (Louvre, Paris).

The question becomes even more insistent when one reflects on the tone and spirit of Rosso's drawing. Carroll has defined this as "mock serious," a response elaborated by John Shearman: "The subject itself is mocked. . . . Mars is revealed by Cupid as improbably triumphant and anything but master of the situation. What the work stimulates positively is not belief in a narrative, not the evocation of something real outside of itself, but fascination in itself, in its complexities, its visual jokes, its *tours de force* of manipulation and technique, and its accumulated demonstration of artistic capacity."[36] Paul Barolsky has chided Shearman for the elaborate circumlocution that never quite identifies the "visual jokes" that indicate how Mars is "anything but master of the situation." As Barolsky remarks, "Rosso mocks the frail Mars, who is a parody of the heroic god of war,"[37] doing so primarily through the visual joke that his *designo* places almost at the focal point of the drawing. In graphic contrast to the ithyphallic satyrs and Priapi that would come to ornament Fontainebleau, this reluctant Mars is anything but ready for his Venereal encounter. Specifically, the joke is the abnormal tininess of his genitals, which are represented as virtually identical in size to those of the prepubescent Cupid, here a boy half the size of Mars. The joke is underscored by the putto in the center foreground, who has placed Mars's naked weapon between his own legs.[38] In opposition to the Neoplatonic allegorization of the myth favored earlier by the Ficino circle,[39] this conquest of Mars is unavoidably literal: he is unmanned by Venus.

What kind of thing is *that* to say about a prince? An impossibility, some art historians have concluded. Writing independently of Barolsky, Graham Smith comments on the same details—the dominance of the female figure and the indication of Mars's sexual incapacity by "a miniaturization of crucial parts." His reading of the tone, however, leads him to reject the topical dimension: " . . . if the mockery, wry humor, and irreverence are aimed primarily at Mars, the idea of identifying Francis I with Mars becomes unlikely."[40] Eugene Carroll, responding to the arguments of Sherman, Barolsky, and Smith, now believes that accepting Adhémar's thesis requires him to recant his earlier description of the tone as "mock serious." Instead, he asserts that Rosso's technical accomplishment in projecting the "feelings and attitudes of others" results in "an experience of a different order of seriousness."[41] Nonetheless, if Aretino did guide Rosso to an attitude toward the royal wedding, it is difficult to elevate the seriousness above the mockery in its expression.

Whether through uncanny prescience or because life does follow art, what Rosso's drawing says about the prince is apparently accurate. By 1532 Marguerite de Navarre could comment to the Duke of Norfolk that for the past seven months her brother had not had conjugal relations with Eleanor:

"he neither lay with her, nor yet meddled with her." Doubtless astonished at this reversal of form by the amorous Francis, Norfolk asked the reason for his behavior. Marguerite replied, " 'She is very hot in bed, and desireth to be too much embraced;' and therewith she fell upon a great laughter, saying, 'I would [not] for all the good in Paris that the king of Navarre were [no be]tter pleased to be in my bed than my brother is to be [in hers.']"[42] Marguerite's "great laughter" at her brother's discomfiture is, indeed, a different order of seriousness.

Rosso's drawing initiated an unusual motif in Fontainebleau art, one that was developed largely by his compatriot assistants, Luca Penni and Francesco Primaticcio, the latter succeeding Rosso as the primary artist in the project. Emerging as the dominant figure in the massive and complex decorative plan perhaps even before Rosso's death, Primaticcio, in particular, was responsible for its sensual glorification of the human body and the highly individualistic treatment of the female nude. Zerner observes that "few types of art have been capable of such a rich eroticism; the licentious extravagance of the pictures is . . . shielded by the decorative significance, always richly charged with motifs."[43] Christopher Marlowe could have been describing Fontainebleau when he wrote: "There might you see the gods in sundrie shapes, / Committing headdie ryots, incest, rapes." Yet, among the endless mythological studies flatteringly alluding to Francis as a Jupiter taking his pleasures, a Ulysses come home, a conquering Alexander, or a Mars, not to mention the more general expressions of masculine sexual imperialism—the voyeuristic sequence of nude bathing scenes for the Appartement des Bains or the recurrent decorative motif of satyrs ravishing nymphs—there emerges an odd, minor strand emphasizing the sexual reversals of Rosso's paradigmatic Mars and Venus: aggressive, emasculating women and impotent men.

The dangerously easy reversibility of sexual roles is underscored by a pair of etchings (figs. 5 and 6), signed "L.D." (Leon Daven?), from Primaticcio drawings: in one, two nude women carry another, apparently reluctant, naked woman to a sexually aroused satyr, who rather incongruously sits on the edge of a cushioned bed; in the other, two grinning satyrs carry an ithyphallic, but nonetheless protesting, satyr to an aroused woman, the position of whose spread legs duplicates that of the receptive satyr in the first. Although the stylization of the figures makes it impossible to be certain, the actors may be the same.

The Mars and Venus myth continues to serve as an expression of feminine sexual aggression in other renderings. Antonio Fantuzzi's etching (fig. 7) of another Primaticcio drawing shows the two bathing. A boyish and beardless Mars—resembling, like Rosso's, the conventional Adonis—already is in the wooden tub, visible only from the chest upward. He extends an

5. "L.D.," *Nude Woman Carried to a Satyr* (Bibliothèque Nationale, Paris).

6. "L.D.," *Satyr Carried to a Woman* (Bibliothèque Nationale, Paris).

arm to steady Venus as she discards her robe while stepping into the tub. Despite Mars's intimate grasp of her inner thigh, Venus once again is the dominant figure. Her full-length, visually commanding body is poised to express strength and energy; outside the bath, beneath Mars's recessive figure, a discarded sword makes the usual phallic joke.

An etching (fig. 8) from a design possibly by Penni acts as a witty "After" to Rosso's "Before." Mars is discovered sleeping as Venus lifts the drapery hanging above the bed and Cupid tries vainly to arouse the hero. The disarray of Venus's coiffure (an unusual touch in a Fontainebleau nude) and the exaggerated disorder of the bed covering, a twist of which is knotted about Mars's right thigh in the conventional sign of bondage to love,[44] assure the beholder that the battle has been fought and lost. The joke is that the exhausted Mars feigns sleep to escape another skirmish; because his head is turned away from Venus and Cupid, they do not see that his eyes are open. At Venus's feet, mimicking her watchful stance, sits a cat, a beast known as lustful and a cruel predator.[45]

Some of the scenes reveal a preoccupation with lesbianism. Jean Mignon's splendid etching (fig. 9) from another Penni drawing depicts a dozen nude women bathing in a sumptuous Roman pool. Right of center, two women seated on the edge of the pool caress sexually while watching their reflection in a mirror held before them by a third. Zerner remarks that "there is no apparent mythological pretext for this slightly licentious glorification of the pleasures of the bath."[46] It might be argued that the composition simply caters to male fantasies, but in the context developed here, the scene can be read plausibly as a myth of female sexual empowerment. Sexually self-sufficient, these women create their own, exclusively female, world of pleasure—even the servants are women. Not just marginalized, men are nonexistent. What is more threatening than to cease to be?

More enigmatic is the Pierre Milan engraving (fig. 10). of Primaticcio's *Jupiter and Callisto,* which illustrates the moment when Jupiter, having taken on the shape of Diana, kisses the nymph *"nec moderata satis nec sic a virgine danda,"* as Ovid says in the *Metamorphoses* (2.431). To the right, Cupid aims an arrow at Callisto; to the left, a pair of putti (possibly Eros and Anteros) eye each other. A mask at Cupid's feet warns of the deception and an eagle signals Jupiter's identity. Diana-Jupiter kisses Callisto openmouthed, aggressively fondling her naked breast and parting her legs with one of his. Despite the mythological trappings, the obvious interest of the composition lies in the eroticism of two physically attractive and revealingly draped women making love. To register Jupiter's presence is not to counteract that first impression but only to complicate it. Do we have the delights of transvestism suggested? Or the pictorial assertion that female erotic plea-

114

7. Antonio Fantuzzi, *Mars and Venus Bathing* (Bibliothèque Nationale, Paris).

8. "L.D.," *Mars, Venus, and Cupid* (Albertina, Vienna).

9. Jean Mignon, *Women Bathing* (Bibliothèque Nationale, Paris).

10. Pierre Milan, *Jupiter and Calisto* (Albertina, Vienna).

sure transcends that of the gods? However we read the scene, once again the male role is diminished or eclipsed by female dominance.

Primaticcio also drew versions of the two standard scenes that depict the myth of Hercules' enslavement to Omphale. One represents the episode wherein Pan, who has fallen in love with Omphale, enters her chamber and, deceived by Hercules' feminine attire, climbs into bed with him. Primaticcio illustrates the moment at which Omphale's servants enter the chamber with a torch to find their mistress awakened beside the disgusted Hercules, who has tossed the confused satyr to the floor.[47] The other, sufficiently popular to have been made a print twice (Zerner, A.F. 17, and fig. 11), shows Omphale establishing her domination through the exchange of costumes. A half dozen nearly naked attendants gather round the towering central figures; Omphale, grotesquely wearing the lion's skin over her head, works to install the hero in his new female garment. Once again the theme is drawn out by a visual joke: Hercules' gaze is directed toward the herm of a satyr, rather resembling himself, that is pointedly not ithyphallic. Sylvie Béguin has noted the topical implication: "il ferait allusion à l'amour conjugal de François Ier et de la reine Éléonore."[48]

The final example, a Primaticcio drawing (fig. 12), puts the matter so directly that little elaboration is necessary. A satyr lies on his back on a makeshift bed or altar before a curtained backdrop. His arms are stretched over his head, his wrists bound to a vine stock, and his body contorted. A businesslike nymph pinions his right leg with her body and his left over her shoulder as she emasculates him with a curved pruning knife. The bunch of grapes hanging from the vine may indicate that she is a Bacchante. In the central foreground, directly in line with the satyr's phallus, a cut stump makes the obvious symbolic commentary.

Admittedly, the strand of mythological art isolated here constitutes a minor element in the prodigality of the artistic productivity sponsored by Francis. But it seems undeniable that the gamble by Aretino and Rosso paid off. The Mars and Venus drawing struck a chord in Francis, one that was exploited thereafter by Primaticcio and Penni. We can only assume that the king gave them license to do so; the compositions appealed to him in some way.

John Pope-Hennessy has reflected on the difficulty of reconstructing sexual attitudes in a distant culture. Considering the matter of Cellini's 1557 conviction for sodomy, he observes:

> From the prevailing legislation, it might be supposed that sexual deviance was the subject of strong social disapproval and was rigorously discouraged by the state. But the facts were very different. Cinquecento life seems gener-

11. "L.D.," *Hercules and Omphale* (Albertina, Vienna).

12. "L.D.," *Nymph Mutilating a Satyr* (École des Beaux-Arts, Paris).

ally to have conformed to a bisexual norm. Cellini's *Life* contains repeated references to sexual relations with female models, and he also had relations with male members of his staff. Such relations were not strongly disapproved of, and were not subject to legal action unless some denunciation, malicious or otherwise, was made.[49]

Pope-Hennessy further cites the example of the *letterato* Benedetto Varchi, who, though he had a series of liaisons with his well-born pupils, was prosecuted only once, for seducing a young girl. "His behavior was seemingly regarded as a legal misdemeanor, to which no moral stigma was attached, and . . . his public life proceeded on the same lines as before."[50] To this we might add the case of Aretino, whose love life was certainly bisexual; although he wrote a sonnet proclaiming that Isabella Sforza had converted him from homosexuality, it appears that he was later obliged to flee Venice to avoid a charge of sodomy.[51]

Such examples do suggest that, whatever the legal and moral attitudes toward ordinary citizens, bisexuality was tolerated, accepted, and perhaps taken for granted among artists, writers, scholars, and the nobles who were their patrons. A telling illustration occurs in Cellini's *Life*, after his departure from France and return to Florence under the patronage of Cosimo I. A bitter quarrel between Cellini and his rival, Bandinelli, erupted before the duke and his courtiers. At the climax of the unpleasant scene Bandinelli called Cellini a "dirty sodomite," provoking this response: "You madman, you're going too far. But I wish to God I did know how to indulge in such a noble practice; after all, we read that Jove enjoyed it with Ganymede in paradise, and here on earth it is the practice of the greatest emperors and the greatest kings of the world. I'm an insignificant, humble man, I haven't the means or the knowledge to meddle in such a marvellous matter."[52] Almost as interesting as the retort are the reaction of the court—"the Duke and the others raised a great shout of laughter which shook the whole place"—and Cellini's interpretation of the incident: "But for all that I took the incident jokingly . . . it was the Duke, not me, whom he insulted."[53] Significantly, the shouting match began with Bandinelli's pique at Cellini's offer to restore a damaged antique statue, the torso of a boy, by transforming it into a Ganymede.[54] Surely Cellini does not mean that Cosimo I was insulted by having homosexuality mentioned in his presence, nor—given the Duke's reaction—could Bandinelli's slur possibly be meant to suggest a sexual relationship between Cosimo and his artist. Rather, the frustrated rival makes an ill-timed attack on the patronage system, reducing it to a demeaning sexual connection. Cellini is quick-witted enough to expand the sexual metaphor, renewing its social potential. In this exposition the artist is no godlike creator. Depreciating himself as humble, ignorant, and insignificant, he confers easy divinity on the kings and emperors who sponsor him. Thus plumping Cosimo's ego, Cellini patches the rip in the social fabric that the inept Bandinelli has torn.

James M. Saslow argues "that in Cellini's time the social patterns connecting men and boys tended to follow classical models, and that many Renaissance men were sexually attracted to youths rather than to men of their own age."[55] He is correct in seeing the importance of classical models for sexual behavior; the gifts of humanism went beyond rhetoric and style. But, as Aretino, Varchi, and Cellini witness, that heritage is described more accurately as bisexual than as homosexual. In a very suggestive study, "Homosexuality in Ancient Rome," Paul Veyne surveys the evidence from a pantheon of Latin authors familiar to any good humanist and concludes with epigrammatic succinctness: "To be active was to be male, whatever the sex of the compliant partner. To take one's pleasure was virile, to accept it servile—that was the whole story."[56]

In the sixteenth-century circles we have been examining, as in classical Rome, no blame attaches to the active partner in a homosexual relationship; and, Saslow agrees, "Those who, like Aretino, were actively bisexual saw no shame in seducing both women and boys, so long as in both cases they consistently played the active part as did the king of the gods in his bisexual affairs."[57] The difficulty arises with that metaphoric extension of the model from sex to art. The bullying Aretino—perhaps significantly a writer rather than an artist—seems unique in his ability to approach patrons as an equal. The more typical pattern emerges in Cellini's revealing anecdote: this intensely virile swashbuckler must play the woman's part with Cosimo I, soothing, flattering, amusing, subordinating himself. In the hierarchy of the court, only the prince can be always dominant.

It may be no oversimplification to conclude that, for Cinquecento culture, the behavioral antimonies of active versus passive and dominant versus subordinate can be subsumed in the categories of masculine and feminine. Saslow sees Castiglione's *Cortegiano* as linking homosexuality with effeminacy because such assumptions about gender are taken for granted by the speakers: "Underlying the otherwise divergent opinions about ideal behavior runs the shared notion of a fundamental polarity between men and women. Men are by nature active, women passive; strong men perform actions, weak women are acted upon."[58] Quoting the archsexist Gasparo on the inherent imperfection of women, he observes that, "except to moderate the harshness of his value judgment, no one disputes Gasparo Pallavicino's theory,"[59] but this is certainly inaccurate. To Gasparo's further argument that women's imperfection causes them to seek the perfection of men, Giuliano de' Medici quickly rebuts, "The poor creatures do not desire to be men in order to become more perfect, but in order to gain freedom and to escape that rule over them which man has arrogated to himself by his own authority."[60] Scholars who have examined Castiglione in the context of the contemporary *querelle des femmes* seem to agree: "There can be no doubt that here and elsewhere the *Courtier* asserts the dignity of women and their essential equality with men."[61]

Rather, Gasparo's function in the dialogues is to represent the opinions of the world outside the court of Urbino, an intrusion of hostile reality into the idealization. His role of licensed social critic, like that of the court fool, exists through the indulgence of the ruler, in this case a ruler whose very presence upsets the expected social hierarchy. In the *Courtier* the invalid Duke Guidobaldo remains only a respectfully mentioned name. As far as the book is concerned, the duchess is the true power of the court, implementing her authority through her lively sister-in-law, Emilia Pia; and on one occasion, when Pallavicino exceeds the limits, "at a signal from the Duchess" the court ladies "all rushed laughing upon signor Gasparo as if to assail him with blows and treat him as the bacchantes treated Orpheus."[62] Wayne Rebhorn no doubt rightly attributes Gasparo's antagonism to his resentment of the unusual social structure, suggesting further that the "hostile reaction to women's social power also reveals a definite fear of female sexuality."[63] The allusions to effeminacy or homosexuality are made humorously or condescendingly, but Gasparo's own anxieties seem to surface in a bitter diatribe against the Petrarchan lady:

> ... still they relish the torment of their lover, because they think that pain and afflictions and the constant invocation of death is the true sign that they are loved, and that by their beauty they can make men miserable or happy, and bestow life and death upon them as they choose. Hence, they feed only on this food, and are so greedy of it that in order not to be without it they neither content their lovers nor reduce them to utter despair; but, in order to keep them continually in worries and in desire, they resort to a certain domineering austerity in the form of threats mingled with hope, and expect a word of theirs, a look, a nod, to be deemed the highest happiness.[64]

As Gasparo's language makes clear (*"una certa imperiosa austerità"*), this is sexual politics with a vengeance, and his indignation at the unaccustomed role reversal—the virile courtier now servilely dancing attendance at the lady's pleasure—again confirms the pervasive stereotypes of accepted masculine and feminine behavior.[65]

After this lengthy circumnavigation, it should be possible to return to our subject, the Bellin da Modena mythological portrait of Francis I, with a firmer sense of context. There are so many questions concerning the provenance of this work that it is impossible to speak in certainties. If the attribution to Niccolò Bellin da Modena is correct, the date and locus remain conjectural. Art historians have proposed 1545, which Johnson accepts because of the proximity to the 1552 medallic adaptation.[66] Yet Martin Biddle's painstaking reconstruction of Bellin da Modena's career indicates that at this time he was engaged on the decoration of Nonsuch Palace and Henry VIII's tomb. After having become involved in a scheme to defraud the French state, he fled to England in 1537 and seems to have remained there until his death in 1569.[67] Why should Bellin da Modena have painted a portrait "idealizing" the monarch who attempted twice, once in 1538 and again in 1540, to have him extradited on criminal charges? How did the portrait return to France to become the model for the medal reverse?[68] Precisely because of these uncertainties in provenance, it becomes the more important to understand the portrait by establishing the appropriate interpretative context.

Looked at in context, the portrait appears very much a part of the line established by Rosso's *Mars and Venus.* The ostensible subject, a glorified, godlike Francis I, emerges rather as an unmanned Mars, a Hercules in Omphale's dress. In it the monarch, whose personal life was dominated successively by mother and mistress, sees a mirror of his public humiliation. Although the prince heads the pecking order of his own court, he himself is subject to the authority of a superior prince. The defeat at Pavia and the subsequent imprisonment had the effect of placing Charles V's foot on Francis's neck, a situation that was symbolically replicated when, his mother and his aunt having concluded the "Peace of the Ladies," he was forced to accept the sister of his conqueror as his wife. Publicly subordinated to the emperor, Francis surrendered his active role in western European power politics and occupied himself with the pursuit of arts patronage. Castiglione's ideal courtier is accomplished in the fine arts and in letters as a complement to his martial and chivalric skills, but not as a primary activity. Gasparo Pallivicino's strictures on musicianship doubtless extend to the other arts as well: "I think that music, along with many other vanities, is indeed well suited to women, and perhaps also to others who have the appearance of men, but not to real men; for the latter ought not to render their minds effeminate and afraid of death."[69] Outside Castiglione's fictive Urbino and Francis's invented Fontainebleau there was a world crowded with Pallivicinos, as both must have been aware. In short, the bisexuality of Bellin da Modena's human deity is not the self-sufficient integration of the androgyne but the impotent neutrality of Hermaphroditus.[70]

As with the emblems being created in this same time period, the meaning of the portrait emerges from an interaction between word and picture, although the relation here is one of counterpoint, rather than the mutual amplification of the emblem.[71] Given the explanatory poem, the quality of the humor might be defined best by recourse to an explanation of verbal humor and its strategies contemporary to the painting. Castiglione's Book II advances the proposition that the courtier should be able to "move [people] to gaiety and laughter with amusing witticisms and pleasantries";[72] the assignment to discourse on this art is given to Bernardo da Bibbiena, author of the comedy *Calandria*.

Freely adapting from the discussion of joking in Cicero's *De oratore*, Castiglione has Bibbiena divide jokes, like Caesar's Gaul, into three provinces—festive or urbane narrations, brief witticisms (*detti* or *arguzie*) and practial jokes (*burle*)[73] The second of these bulks much the largest, but the categories tend to overlap because the quality of humor most prized remains a constant. Bibbiena defines man as a "risible animal" and believes that what makes the animal laugh is the exploitation of verbal ambiguity in any form. Puns, plays on words, the deliberate misuse of quotations, saying one thing while meaning another, and euphemisms are all favored devices for speakers, just as twisting another's words, accepting them in a way not anticipated, turning his metaphor against him, or replying in an unexpected way are approved retorts.

Ambiguity—sexual ambiguity—is the overriding joke of the portrait, but the rhetorical devices enumerated and illustrated by Bibbiena prove useful in considering the strategies of the verses. The opening line, *"FRancoys en guerre est un Mars furieux,"* establishes the basic technique. Bibbiena comments both on comparisons as a source of humor and on the use of overstatement, as when "we say things that exceed verisimilitude in some incredible way."[74] Nonetheless, it is suavely done, offering praise that elsewhere might be accepted at face value. Francis's courage in battle was beyond dispute: like Shakespeare's Richard III, when captured at Pavia he was fighting valiantly on foot after his horse had been killed. But the defeat and captivity are events that cannot be blinked away. No god, only a fallible mortal.

"En paix Minerve & diane a la chasse." Again, the comparisons are apt and deserved up to a point. By all accounts Francis was passionately devoted to hunting, and Diana became one of the resident genii of Fontainebleau well before Diane de Poitiers became his son Henri's mistress. A verse on the engraving of Rosso's celebrated *Nymph of Fontainebleau* apostrophizes, "Franciscus primus, Francorum Rex potentiss bonarum artium ac literarum pater, sub Diana, a venatu conquiescentis" (Zerner, P.M. 7). Similarly, as the embodiment of wisdom and the patron of arts and letters, Minerva makes an apt comparison. Given the gender attitudes prevailing in the culture, however, her role as a war goddess becomes rather more problematic. Yet more overtly inappropriate, the primary characteristic of both virgin goddesses is their fierce dedication to chastity. Here we encounter the joke "in

which there is a hidden meaning quite different from the one we seem to intend," the "nice sort of pleasantry . . . which consists in a certain dissimulation, when one thing is said and another is tacitly understood."[75]

If the first three gods evoke a mixture of the positive and the negative, the final pair project a seemingly unqualified positive-negative polarity. *"A bien parler Mercure copieux"* appears to be unconditionally apposite and laudatory. Francis was noted for his personal charm, affability, courtesy, agreeable conversation, and eloquence, and Mercury's roles as patron of arts and learning and as guide to travelers render him a fit image for the royal patron who guided the Italian Renaissance to France. Conversely, *"A bien aymer vray Amour plein de grace"* strikes an incongruous note. The Neoplatonic systemization and idealization of love had long since become familiar in French court circles, but the decidedly antiplatonic, amorous behavior of Francis subverts the possibility of an unequivocal identification with Ficino's cosmic principle.[76] For Francis, "grace" has little to do with Cupid's activities, except in the courtly euphemism for sexual compliance, and the calculated redundancy of verb and noun (*"aymer . . . Amour"*), juxtaposed to the presence of Cupid's traditional enemies, Minerva and Diana, points by innuendo to the king's amorous nature. Because Cupid is the one unexalted and unheroic deity in the catalog, we have here an example of the pleasantry in which "laughter is aroused by saying something contrary to expectation"[77] and perhaps the "ironical" device "in which an evil thing is called by a polite name."[78]

Admittedly, the conventional reading procedure with symbolic attributes is one of selective application: the comparison involves a specific, delimited facet of relationship and one does not expect or seek total correspondence. If the little poem existed independently, such an approach would be possible and appropriate; except for the slightly anomalous *"Amour,"* the rhetoric easily could be read as straightforward glorification. But the portrait militates against such a reading. As I have argued, Bellin da Modena avoids an iconic or emblematic style that would reinforce a literal response to the verses, giving us instead a grotesque naturalism—itself a partial parody of the fashionable style officially sponsored by Francis—that constantly undercuts the hyperbolic comparisons, driving a wedge between image and words to force awareness of the ambiguity and equivocation latent in the praise. Bibbiena's analysis of the origin of humor can serve very well for a final commentary on the bisexual portrait: "Now the place and as it were the source of the laughable consists in a certain deformity, for we laugh only at those things that have incongruity in them and that seem to be amiss and yet are not. . . . what we laugh at is nearly always something incongruous, and yet is not amiss."[79]

Tonally, the Bellin da Modena portrait is much of a piece with Rosso's

Mars and Venus from which it derives conceptually. They are sophisticated "pleasantries," to borrow Castiglione's term, treating their royal subject with mock praise that, although puncturing his dignity, deflating any pretense of infallibility, and calling attention to his human reverses, does so in a good-natured way that nicely judges the limits of Francis's tolerance and does not go "beyond the bounds." That Francis could sponsor art of this character is no little tribute to his own character. These works presuppose an intelligent and witty man who is self-conscious enough to be aware that criticism and satire embraced and diffused into harmless laughter are more easily endured than when hidden beneath a façade of facile praise. There was a tradition of a laughing or witty ruler, deriving from the literature of imperial Rome and cultivated by such Renaissance rulers as Cosimo de' Medici and Alfonso V of Aragon, king of Naples, but an examination of their jokes tends to confirm the impression that the humor is at the expense of others.[80] A prince who amiably allows himself to be the butt of jokes is rather more unusual.

Although the motives for such a course of behavior lie in Francis's psychology, there is some likelihood that he learned the style for implementing them from *The Courtier,* as much a manual for the ideal prince as for the ideal gentleman. The use of Castiglione's strategies of humor to analyze the tone of Bellin da Modena's portrait is not a gratuitous association, for the connections between the imaginary court at Urbino and the real court at Fontainebleau are too dense to dismiss as accidental.

Castiglione and Francis I met twice, in December 1515 at Bologna and nine years later near Pavia. Sometime near the first meeting, Castiglione inserted in the first version of his book the claim that Francis, through the agency of Alfonso Ariosto, had expressed his desire that the work be completed. Shifting political alliances evidently caused this reference to be removed from the *seconda redazione* of 1518–20, but the text published in 1528 includes an encomium of Francis—using the dialogues' fictive date as a point of reference—as a future embodiment of the perfect prince:

> But if kind fate will have it that Monseigneur d'Angoulême succeed to the crown, as is hoped, then I think that just as the glory of arms flourishes and shines in France, so must that of letters flourish there also with the greatest splendor. . . . I saw this prince; and, besides the disposition of his body and the beauty of his countenance, he appeared to me to have in his aspect such greatness (yet joined with a certain gracious humanity) that the realm of France must always seem a petty realm to him.[81]

Yet more tangibly, it has been shown that, in the period immediately following Castiglione's initial meeting with Francis, virtually all the principal male courtiers depicted in the first draft—Lodovico Canossa, Bibbiena,

Giuliano de' Medici, Francesco Maria della Rovere, Federico and Ottaviano Fregoso—had personal contact with the king and obtained his patronage: "Indeed after the meeting at Bologna in December 1515 the extent to which the former courtiers of Urbino acquired royal patronage is remarkable. In a sense the court of Urbino as it existed in 1507, so familiar as a result of Castiglione's portrayal of it on the eve of its disintegration, came to be partially, and only as far as its male members were concerned, regrouped with Francis I as patron."[82] Given this nexus of relation, one can only speculate on the direction in which influences might have flowed. Did Castiglione tailor his manuscript to suit the ideas and style current in the court of the young king? Did Francis hear enough about the work, perhaps even reading it in manuscript, to wish to encourage its actors as well as its author? Did Castiglione's fiction record the real opinions and attitudes of a courtier—Bibbiena, for instance—who also imparted them to Francis? Was Francis sufficiently intrigued by his contacts with this group of courtiers to foster a sustained interest in the book? However one wishes to sort out the possibilities, it is plausible that the consonance of ideas and styles is, to some degree, causal.[83] In all likelihood the association was a matter of general knowledge.

During the autumn of 1529 Rosso Fiorentino, still seeking a safe harbor after the devastation of Rome, apparently began to think seriously about the possibility of attaching himself to the French court. At Arezzo, one of the way stations he passed through before reaching Aretino's Venice, he left behind several books that suggest he was preparing himself for the attempt: Suetonius, Pliny, Vitruvius, and, among these classics, a recent best-seller, Castiglione's *Cortegiano*. [84]

NOTES

For permission to reproduce photographs, I am indebted to the following: Graphische Sammlung Albertina, Vienna; Bibliothèque Nationale, Paris; the Trustees of the British Museum, London; École Nationale Superieure des Beaux-Arts, Paris; Musées Nationaux, Paris, for the Cabinet des Dessins, Louvre; National Gallery of Art, Washington, D.C., Samuel H. Kress Collection.

1. See the biographical note by W. McAllister Johnson in *Fontainebleau: Art in France, 1528–1610,* 2 vols. (Ottawa: National Gallery of Canada, 1973), 2:32. This exhibition catalogue differs in some respects from the original French version, *L'École de Fontainebleau* (Paris: Éditions des Musées Nationaux, 1972), which discusses the portrait attribution. As Johnson remarks, the eighteenth-century attribution to Niccolò dell'Abate undoubtedly arises from confusion generated by the identical Christian names and the coincidence of their both being natives of Modena. See also Françoise Bardon, "Sur un portrait de François Ier," *L'Information d'histoire de*

l'art 8 (1963): 1–7; and Martin Biddle, "Nicholas Bellin da Modena, an Italian Artificer at the Courts of Francis I and Henry VIII," *Journal of the British Archaeological Association* s. 3, 29 (1966): 106–21, for the fullest account of the artist's life.

2. Bardon, "Sur un portrait," 3. See also Johnson's descriptive note in *L'École de Fontainebleau,* no. 27 (not included in the Ottawa catalogue).

3. Bardon, "Sur un portrait," 3–7. On the genres of political spectacle, see Roy Strong, *Art and Power: Renaissance Festivals, 1450–1650* (Woodbridge, Suffolk: Boydell Press, 1984).

4. André Chastel, *The Age of Humanism: Europe 1480–1530,* trans. Katherine M. Delavenay and E. M. Gwyer (London: Thames and Hudson, 1963), 204.

5. Edgar Wind, *Pagan Mysteries in the Renaissance,* rev. ed. (New York: W. W. Norton, 1968), 213–14. See also Anne-Marie Lecoq, *François Ier imaginaire: symbolique et politique a l'aube de la Renaissance francaise* (Paris: Macula, 1987), 405.

6. For Simeoni, see Bardon, "Sur un portrait," 4, fig. 3; and, for Stopio, see Jeromino Ruscelli, *Le imprese illustri* (Venice, 1566), 284–5.

7. See *The Mirrovr of Maiestie: or the Badges of Honovr,* ed. Henry Green and James Croston, Holbein Society (London: Trubner & Co., 1870), emblem 13; and, for the soldier-scholar, emblem 30. On this general topic, see Robert J. Clements, "Pen and Sword," *Picta Poesis: Literary and Humanistic Theory in Renaissance Emblem Books,* Temi e Testi (Rome: Edizioni di storia e letterature, 1960), 6:135–49.

8. For a full description of the medal, see G. F. Hill and Graham Pollard, *Renaissance Medals from the Samuel H. Kress Collection* (London: Phaidon Press, 1967), no. 105. See also Sperandio's medal of Floriano Dolfi in G. F. Hill, *A Corpus of Italian Medals of the Renaissance before Cellini* (London: British Museum, 1930), no. 387. The Janiform figure of the reverse apparently alludes to Dolfi's religious and secular offices.

9. On this medal, see Mark Jones, *A Catalogue of the French Medals in the British Museum: Volume 1, AD 1402–1610* (London: British Museum, 1982), no. 62; W. McAllister Johnson, "Numismatic Propaganda in Renaissance France," *Art Quarterly* 31 (1968): 123–51; and a forthcoming study by Ralph E. Giesey. Johnson correctly describes the medal as a "modification" of the painting ("Numismatic," 139); Lecoq, refers to the figures as if they were the same (*François Ier,* 405). The attribution is problematic: Mazerolle assigned it to Marc Bechot; Jones inclines toward Etienne Delaune; and Giesey will present a new candidate (see note 68 below). I am indebted to Mark Jones for allowing me to examine the British Museum specimen, as well as for helpful discussion of it. The allegorical figure also appears as the reverse to a 1552 medal with an obverse bust of Henri II. See Johnson, "Numismatic," figs. 23 and 24; and Fernand Mazerolle, *Les médailleurs francais du XVe au milieu du XVIIe siècle* 3 vols. (Paris: Imprimerie nationale, 1902–4), nos. 89–90.

10. Anne Hollander, *Seeing through Clothes* (New York: Viking Press, 1978), 98. See also pp. 96–112 for her interesting discussion, on which this paragraph relies.

11. Ibid. 98.

12. On the *linea* or *figura serpentinata,* see David Summers, *Michelangelo and the Language of Art* (Princeton: Princeton University Press, 1981), 82–3; and *The School of Fontainebleau: An Exhibition* (Fort Worth Art Center and University Art Museum, University of Texas, 1965), 19–20.

13. See R. J. Knecht, *Francis I* (Cambridge: Cambridge University Press, 1982), 86, 426–29. For the fullest review of this issue in an attempt to restore Francis's reputation, see Paulin Paris, *Études sur François premier*, 2 vols., ed. Gaston Paris (Paris: L. Techener, 1885).

14. Quoted in Knecht, *Francis I*, 86.

15. Quoted in Knecht, "The Court of Francis I," *European Studies Review* 8 (1978): 15–16. He comments, "Could anything express more eloquently the courtier's contempt for his social inferiors?"

16. Quoted in Knecht, *Francis I*, 428.

17. Ibid. 86, 416–19.

18. Quoted in Knecht, *Francis I*, 428 n.

19. Jules Michelet, *Histoire de France au seizième siècle*, in *Oeuvre Complètes*, gen. ed. Paul Viallaneix, 21 vols., *Renaissance Reforme*, ed. Robert Casanova, (Paris: Flammarion, 1978), 7:228.

20. Quoted in Knecht, *Francis I*, 192.

21. On the regency, see Knecht, *Francis I*, 176–205; and, for the treaty of Cambrai, 219–20. See also John F. Freeman, "Louise of Savoy: A Case of Maternal Opportunism," *Sixteenth Century Journal* 3 (1972): 77–98.

22. Quoted in Knecht, *Francis I*, 192.

23. Quoted in Knecht, *Francis I*, 237, from *State Papers of Henry VIII*, 11 vols. (London: Her Majesty's Stationery Office, 1830–52), 7:291.

24. For details, see Knecht, *Francis I*, 192–93, 422–23.

25. André Chastel, "Fontainebleau: Forms and Symbols," in *Fontainebleau: Art in France, 1528–1610*, 1: 235.

26. On Francis as a collector, see Knecht, *Francis I*, 264–68; Jean Adhemar, "The Collection of Francis the First," *Gazette des Beaux-Arts*, 6th series, 30 (1946): 5–16; Janet Cox-Rearick, *La collection de François Ier* (Paris: Éditions des musées nationaux, 1972); Francis Haskell and Nicholas Penny, *Taste and the Antique* (New Haven: Yale University Press, 1981), chap. 1.

27. Dora and Erwin Panofsky have argued the presence of a coherent and consistent iconographic program in "The Iconography of the Galerie François Ier at Fontainebleau," *Gazette des Beaux-Arts*, 6th ser., 52 (1958): 113–90; but see the qualifications made in *Revue de l'Art*, special number 16–17 (1972).

28. On the importance of the print workshop, ca. 1542–48, see Chastel, "Forms and Symbols," 239–40; and, especially, Henri Zerner, *The School of Fontainebleau: Etchings and Engravings* (New York: Harry N. Abrams, 1969).

29. Sam Cantey III, in *The School of Fontainebleau: An Exhibition*, 19–20.

30. Chastel, "Forms and Symbols," 245.

31. Zerner, *Etchings*, 11.

32. See Jean Adhémar, "Aretino: Artistic Adviser to Francis I," *Journal of the Warburg and Courtauld Institutes* 17 (1954): 311–18. For the fullest account of the drawing and a comparison to the later print, see Eugene A. Carroll, *The Drawings of Rosso Fiorentino*, Outstanding Dissertations in the Fine Arts, 2 vols. (New York: Garland, 1976), 2: 322–38; and, most recently, *Rosso Fiorentino: Drawings, Prints, and Decorative Arts* (Washington: National Gallery of Art, 1987), 170–75, 176–79. See also Sylvie Béguin in *L'École de Fontainebleau*, 181, no. 204.

33. I quote Carroll's translation from "Rosso in France," in *Actes du colloque international sur l'art de Fontainebleau*, ed. André Chastel (Paris: Centre National de la Recherche Scientifique, 1975), 17.

34. Adhémar, "Aretino," 313.

35. Carroll, "Rosso in France," 19. For Rosso's style at this time, see Sydney J. Freedberg, "Rosso's Style in France and its Italian Context," *Actes du colloque international*, 13–16.

36. John Shearman, *Mannerism* (Harmondsworth: Penguin, 1967), 68. Carroll's phrase occurs in *Drawings*, 1: 218.

37. Paul Barolsky, *Infinite Jest: Wit and Humor in Italian Renaissance Art* (Columbia: University of Missouri Press, 1978), 113.

38. Barolsky notes this point. See Barolsky, *Infinite*, 113–15.

39. On this, see Wind, *Pagon*, 85–96.

40. Graham Smith, "Bronzino's Use of Prints: Some Suggestions," *The Print Collector's Newsletter* 9, no. 4 (1978): 110–13 and n.7.

41. Carroll, *Rosso Fiorentino*, 173. He observes, "It is true that Rosso's Mars has small genitals, but so do most of his male figures" (175, n. 6). Granted, but here the miniaturization is both extreme (compare, e.g., nos. 8a, 14, 27, 39, and 45 in Carroll's catalogue) and pointedly emphasized by Cupid's parallel stance and anatomy. Carroll accepts Smith's suggestion of a relationship to Sodoma's fresco of the *Marriage of Roxana and Alexander* in the Villa Farnesina (*Rosso Fiorentino*, 172), the decorative program of which Pietro Aretino is believed to have influenced. It may be relevant to mention the notorious phallic joke in Giovanni da Udine's decoration of the Cupid and Psyche loggia. See Roger Jones and Nicholas Penny, *Raphael* (New Haven: Yale, 1983), 184–5 and pl. 196. (I owe this reference to Professor Thomas P. Roche, Jr.) For Aretino's personal exploitation of phallic imagery, see R. B. Waddington, "A Satirist's *Impresa:* The Medals of Pietro Aretino," *Renaissance Quarterly*, 52 (1989): 655–81.

42. Quoted in Knecht, *Francis I*, 238.

43. Zerner, *Etchings*, 12. Noting the "marked preference" for Greek subjects over Roman, with their imperial connotations, he further comments, "One feels constantly behind these choices the shadow of the conflict with the Emperor Charles V, which was the main preoccupation of François I's reign."

44. See, for example, Veronese's *Mars and Venus* (Wind, *Pagan*, fig. 76) where Cupid binds the lovers' legs with a ribbon; and Jean Mignon's print (Zerner, *Etchings*, plate J.M. 38), possibly after Penni, in which Cupid binds Venus to Mars's invisible supporting leg.

45. See, for example, Topsell's *Histories of Beasts*, ed. Malcolm South (Chicago: Nelson-Hall, 1981), 37–40. Edward Topsell's *The History of Four-Footed Beasts* (1607) depends largely on Gesner's *Historia animalium* and the standard classical sources.

46. *Fontainebleau*, 2: 96, no. 415.

47. Zerner, *Etchings*, plate L.D. 9. All references herein to reproductions in Zerner are made with the artist's initials and Zerner's plate number.

48. Sylvie Béguin, in *L'École de Fontainebleau*, 139, no. 146.

49. John Pope-Hennessy, *Cellini* (New York: Abbeville Press, 1985), 254.

50. Ibid. 255.

51. The sonnet is quoted in James M. Saslow, *Ganymede in the Renaissance: Homosexuality in Art and Society* (New Haven: Yale University Press, 1986), 72. On the conjectural sodomy charge, see Patricia H. Labalme, "Personality and Politics in Venice: Pietro Aretino," in *Titian: His World and His Legacy*, ed. David Rosand (New York: Columbia University Press, 1982), 124.

52. *The Autobiography of Benvenuto Cellini*, trans. George Bull (Harmondsworth: Penguin, 1956), 338.

53. Ibid.

54. For an analysis of this work, emphasizing the contemporary erotic connotations of the myth, see Saslow, *Ganymede*, 145–51.

55. Ibid. 156.

56. Paul Veyne, "Homosexuality in Ancient Rome," in *Western Sexuality: Practice and Precept in Past and Present Times*, ed. Philippe Ariès and André Béjin, trans. Anthony Forster (Oxford: Basil Blackwell, 1985), 29–30; see also 26–29, 30–35.

57. Saslow, *Ganymede*, 84.

58. Ibid. 81.

59. Ibid.

60. Baldassare Castiglione, *The Book of the Courtier*, trans. Charles S. Singleton (Garden City, N.Y.: Doubleday/Anchor Books, 1959), 217.

61. Dain A. Trafton, "Politics and the Praise of Women," in *Castiglione: The Ideal and the Real in Renaissance Culture*, ed. Robert W. Hanning and David Rosand (New Haven: Yale University Press, 1983), 33. See also J. R. Woodhouse, *Baldesar Castiglione: A Reassessment of "The Courtier"* (Edinburgh: Edinburgh University Press, 1978), 109–36. Joan Kelly concedes the overtly favorable treatment of women, but insists there is covert subordination. See "Did Women Have a Renaissance?" in *Women, History, and Theory: The Essays of Joan Kelly* (Chicago: University of Chicago Press, 1984), 39–47.

62. Castiglione, *Courtier*, 193–94.

63. Wayne Rebhorn, *Courtly Performances: Masking and Festivity in Castiglione's "Book of the Courtier"* (Detroit: Wayne State University Press, 1978), 128. See also his discussion, 126–29.

64. *The Courtier*, 278–9; quoted in Rebhorn, *Courtly Performance*, 128–9.

65. Joan Kelly argues ("Did Women," 44–46) that Castiglione's paradigm of the courtier's relation to the prince is essentially feminine: pleasing, pliant, accommodating, dependent. If so, Gasparo's rejection of courtliness figures a hostility to the changing political situation, "that general restructuring of social relations . . . as feudal independence and reciprocity yielded to the state" (Kelly, "Did Women," 45).

66. See *L'École de Fontainebleau*, 27.

67. See Biddle, "Nicholas Bellin," 109–17. A record of Bellin da Modena's 1552 New Year's gift to Edward VI survives: "a feire picture paynted of the Frenche King his hoole personage, sett in a frame of wood" (Biddle, "Nicholas Bellin," 117); but the date makes it improbable that this was the Francis I portrait. Given that Edward's investiture in the Order of St. Michael occurred in July 1551, the subject is more likely Henri II.

68. Professor Ralph E. Giesey informs me (personal correspondence) that he

has discovered the original of the Henri II medal, which he believes to have been made in England. He describes the bisexual portrait as conjoined with a satiric obverse. These circumstances seem to strengthen the likelihood that Bellin da Modena executed the Francis I portrait in England and that a contemporary understood it as less than wholly serious.

69. Castiglione, *Courtier,* 75.

70. A similar construction could be placed even on Francis's impresa of the salamander in fire: "Fraunces the first . . . who as his slipperie youth did leade him, chaunged the manly exploits of warre, with the weake pleasures and effeminate delights of his fond loue. And to signifie that he fried in these passionat flames, wherein so much he gloried that he shamed not to saie, that he nourished himselfe in them." Samuel Daniel, *The Worthy Tract of Paulus Jovius* (London, 1585), C ii. For the somewhat less pointed original, see Paolo Giovio, *Dialogo dell'imprese militari et amorose* (Lyons, 1574), 29. On the impresa itself, see André Chastel, "La salamandre," *Revue de l'Art,* special number 16–17 (1972): 150–2; and Lecoq, *François Ier,* especially 35–52 and 459–465.

71. On the early development of the emblem, see Hessel Miedema, "The Term *Emblema* in Alciati," *Journal of the Warburg and Courtauld Institutes* 31 (1968): 234–50; and Daniel Russell, "The Term 'Embleme' in Sixteenth-Century France," *Neophilologus* 59 (1975): 336–51.

72. Castiglione, *Courtier,* 140.

73. See *The Courtier,* 141–42, 147. For the use of Cicero, see Georg Luck, " 'Vir Facetus': A Renaissance Ideal," *Studies in Philology* 55 (1958): 121; and Barbara C. Bowen, "Roman Jokes and the Renaissance Prince, 1455–1528," in *Literae Humaniores: Classical Themes in Renaissance Guise,* ed. J. K. Newman, Illinois Classical Studies, 9, no. 2.2 (1984): 146–7. Daniel Javitch comments, "So obvious is the extent of his borrowing that it obscures how much he adapted his source to accommodate it to courtly imperatives." See Javitch, *Poetry and Courtliness in Renaissance England* (Princeton: Princeton University Press, 1978), 34. Also helpful is Robert Grudin, "Renaissance Laughter: The Jests in Castiglione's *Il Cortegiano,*" *Neophilologus* 58 (1974): 199–204.

74. Castiglione, *Courtier,* 165, 168.

75. Ibid. 177, 169.

76. For the transmission of Neoplatonic love theory to France, see Symphorien Champier, *Le livre de vraye amour,* ed. James B. Wadsworth (The Hague: Mouton, 1962); Robert V. Merrill with Robert J. Clements, *Platonism in French Renaissance Poetry* (New York: New York University Press, 1957); A. H. T. Levi, "The Neoplatonist Calculus," *Humanism in France,* ed. A. H. T. Levi (Manchester: Manchester University Press, 1970), 229–48; and Jean Festugiere, *La philosophie de l'amour de Marsile Ficin et son influence sur la litterature francaise au XVIe siècle,* 2nd ed. (Paris: J. Vrin, 1941).

77. Castiglione, *Courtier,* 180.

78. Ibid. 170.

79. Ibid. 145.

80. See Bowen, "Roman Jokes," 137–48.

81. Castiglione, *Courtier,* 67–68.

82. Cecil H. Clough, "Francis I and the Courtiers of Castiglione's *Courtier,*"

European Studies Review 8 (1978): 32–70; quotation, 38. The essay is reprinted in Clough, *The Duchy of Urbino in the Renaissance* (London: Variorum Reprints, 1981).

83. The complete progression may be from fiction to reality to fiction again. See Isida Cremona, "Thélème, *Il Cortegiano* et la cour de François Ier," *Renaissance and Reformation* 14, n.s. 2 (1978): 1–11, for the relationships to Rabelais.

84. See Carroll, *Drawings,* 1: 219–20.

Notes on Contributors

JEAN R. BRINK is professor of English and director of the Arizona Center for Medieval and Renaissance Studies at Arizona State University. She is completing a full-length study of sixteenth-century poetry and politics.

ALLISON COUDERT is lecturer in the Honors College at Arizona State University. Her research interests include the occult and witchcraft.

NANCY GUTIERREZ is associate professor of English at Arizona State University. She is working on a book on adultery in English Renaissance drama.

MARYANNE CLINE HOROWITZ is chair of the History Department at Occidental College and research associate at the UCLA Center for Medieval and Renaissance Studies. She has published widely on ideas of human nature from antiquity through the Renaissance.

MARGARET M. SULLIVAN is completing her dissertation "Gender and Genealogy: From Sidney's *Arcadia* to Richardson's *Pamela*" in the English Department of the University of California, Los Angeles. Her awards include the Lily Bess Campbell (1988–89) and Clark Memorial Library (1989–90) dissertation fellowships.

FUMIKO TAKASE is professor of English and director of the Women's Studies Institute at Kobe College, Japan. Her most recent work involves a study of the *contemptus mundi* topos in Japanese literature.

ALISON TAUFER is assistant professor of English at California State University, Los Angeles. Her work concerns the representation of women and non-Europeans in late Medieval and Renaissance literature.

RAYMOND B. WADDINGTON is professor of English at the University of California, Davis. He is currently working on studies of Pietro Aretino and of Shakespeare's *Sonnets*.

SUSANNE WOODS is dean of the College and vice president for academic affairs at Franklin and Marshall College. She is also director of the Women Writers Project at Brown University.

NAOMI YAVNEH is completing her dissertation "The Threat of Sensuality: Tasso's Temptress and the Counter-Reformation" at the University of California, Berkeley.

Index

Abate, Niccolò dell', 126
Adam, 30, 85, 87–95
Adhémar, Jean, 109, 128n, 129n
Adonis, 109, 112
Adultery, 3–14, 14–18n, 20–21, 24–25, 29, 67
Alchemist, The, 21
Alexander the Great, 112
Alfonso V of Aragon, King of Naples, 125
Alienation, 3–14, 14–18n, 52
Allegory, 21, 53, 89, 94
Amadís Cycle, 35–48, 48–51n
Amadís de Gaule, 70
Amadís de Grecia, 38, 41, 45–47, 49–51n
Amazon basin, 37
Amazons, 35–48, 48–51n, 52–60, 60–61n,
  62–75, 76–81n; annihilation of, 36; con-
  quest of, 36; domination of, 36
America, 57
Androgyny, 71, 88, 89
Anthropomorphism, 86
Antifeminism, 19–30, 30–31n
Appearance vs. reality, 7, 21–29
Aptekar, Jane, 52, 55, 56, 60n, 61n
Aramaic, 91
Arcadia, 62–75, 76–81n
Aretino, Pietro, 108, 109, 111, 117, 120, 126
Arezzo, 126
Aries, Philip, 130n
Ariosto, Alfonso, 125
Aristocracy, 62–75, 76–81n
Aristophanes, 19, 85, 88, 89
Athena, 102
Attica, 36
Audencia, 39
Augustine, Saint, 93, 94, 98n
Authority, 4, 6, 10, 12, 54, 74; usurpation of,
  52
Autonomy, female, 75

Bacon, Francis, 9, 16n

Bandinelli, 119, 120
Baptism, 8, 45, 48; forced, 39, 40
Barbarians, 35–39, 42, 48, 59
Barclay, Alexander, 19, 30n
Bardon, Françoise, 101, 102, 126n, 127n
Barnet, Sylvan, 15n
Barolsky, Paul, 111, 129n
Baughan, Denver, 79n
Beatis, Antonio De, 106
Bechot, Marc, 127n
Béguin, Sylvie, 117, 128n, 129n
Béjin, André, 130n
Bellin da Modena, Niccolò, 99–126,
  126–32n
Berkhofer, Robert F., 49n
Bibbiena, Bernardo da, 123–25
Biddle, Martin, 122, 127n, 130n
Bisexuality, 99–126, 126–32n
Bologna, 125, 126
Boose, Lynda, 5, 15n
Bowen, Barbara C., 131n
Bradbrook, Muriel C., 31n
Brant, Sebastian, 19, 30n
Bridenthal, Renate, 17n
Brosse, Jean de, 107
Bull, George, 130n
Bullinger, Heinrich, 16n
Burghley, Lord, 59

Calandria, 123
California, 38
Callisto, 114
Cambrai, treaty of, 106, 108
Cannibalism, 38, 39
Canossa, Lodovico, 125
Canterbury Tales, The, 30n
Cantey, Sam III, 128n
Carmella, Santino, 96n
Carroll, Eugene A., 109, 111, 128n, 129n,
  132n

135